Advance Praise

"As a fellow veteran, I appreciate the leadership lessons and lived experience Dr. Chaunté Hall brings forward in *SOFT*. Her voice reflects the strength, resilience, and purpose we gain through service—values that continue to shape impactful leadership beyond the uniform."

—JoAnne "Jo" Bass, 19th Chief Master Sergeant of the Air Force

"*SOFT* challenges conventional notions of what it means to be strong, reminding us that vulnerability isn't a flaw—it's the foundation of authentic leadership. This book offers readers a disciplined approach to being resilient, grounded, and open: traits that will help every leader thrive."

—Ron Nirenberg, Mayor of San Antonio (2017–2025)

"In *SOFT*, Dr. Chaunté Hall brings the strength of her military roots, the heart of a servant leader, and the wisdom of lived experience. A proud Air Force veteran and lifelong advocate, she turns vulnerability into power and service into purpose. This book is a powerful testament to the strength found in authenticity, resilience, and compassion."

—Juan G. Ayala, Major General, USMC (Retired)

"This book doesn't just speak to the challenges women face, it offers the tools to rise above them with grace, grit, and soul-deep self-belief."

—Angie Lienert, USAF Veteran,
CEO and Founder of IntelliGenesis LLC

"*SOFT* is a reminder that we don't have to trade our empathy for impact or our grace for grit. Dr. Hall's words echo what many of us have lived: True strength doesn't need to be loud or hardened—it just needs to be real."

—Laura Koerner, Naval Academy Graduate,
Former City Councilwoman, and Veteran Advocate

"*SOFT*—a brilliant and fitting title for Dr. Chaunté Hall's book, perfectly capturing the essence of a woman who embodies strength, optimism, energy, and inspiration. She is not just an exceptional leader, but also a devoted daughter, sister, mother, friend, and wingman. As a father of two daughters, I found the life lessons within Chaunté's story deeply resonant. While this book serves as a powerful, unapologetic guide for women to embrace life on their own terms, its wisdom is equally profound for men. I wholeheartedly recommend *SOFT* to anyone eager to expand their perspectives, integrate transformative life, mindset, and leadership principles into their personal and professional journey, and discover how Dr. Hall's philosophies can empower us to excel at work, at home, and within our communities."

—BOB LaBRUTTA, Major General, USAF (Retired)

SOFT

Stoically Optimistic
Females Triumph

SOFT

*Stoically Optimistic
Females Triumph*

DR. CHAUNTÉ HALL

SOFT
Stoically Optimistic Females Triumph

Copyright © 2025 by Dr. Chaunté Hall

Cover Design by Anton Khodakovsky
Interior Layout and Design by Brittany Becker
Editorial Team: Stephanie Rondeau, Traci Matt, Donnel McLohon, Kiska Carr

ISBNs:
E-book: 979-8-89165-269-9
Paperback: 979-8-89165-270-5
Hardcover: 979-8-89165-271-2

Published by:
Streamline
Kansas City, MO
www.shareyourstory.com

To my Heavenly Father—
for never letting me out of His grasp.

To my father, Dr. Steven Hall, USAF veteran, who inspired the name SOFT
and has chosen me, stood by me, and championed every step I've taken.

To my mother, Darlene Hall, USAF veteran,
whose unwavering love and strength helped shape the woman I've become.

To my brothers, Brandon Hall and Dr. Michael Hall,
fellow USAF veterans and my lifelong supporters.

And to my greatest blessings—Noah and Ariana—
your love inspires me daily to rise, lead, and live this beautiful gift called life.

CONTENTS

FOREWORD

D**R. CHAUNTÉ HALL** is a larger-than-life personality, and she knows absolutely everyone. I'm convinced that if she were ever stranded on a desert island, at least one of the rescue crew would already know her. Probably more than one.

After getting to know her personally, I understand why. She puts her heart and soul into every cause she's passionate about—which is a long and ever-growing list. Like compound interest, her impact multiplies over time and continues to pay dividends for everyone lucky enough to cross her path.

Long before we met, I knew her by reputation. I had seen her presence on social media and heard of her through mutual friends. I knew she was an Air Force veteran, a professor, a nonprofit founder, and a fierce advocate for veterans and military families through Centurion Military Alliance. I knew she was a PhD, a mom, and a force for good. What I didn't know was how deeply authentic she is and how much the real Chaunté surpasses even her remarkable public image.

With Chaunté, it's never about her. It's about others. She builds platforms, makes connections, and shines a light on the causes that matter. She helps people not only to care but also to act.

That's why I was so honored (and a little overwhelmed) when she asked me to write this foreword. This is the book I desperately needed in 1995 when I first enlisted in the Air Force. And to be honest, one I needed to read again now, twice, before writing these words.

Back then, I joined the military to escape a path I didn't want to stay on. I wasn't picky about the specific job, thinking it would be one enlistment and done. The assignment really didn't matter. Twenty-nine years later, I retired after holding some of the most personally and professionally demanding roles in the Air Force: aerospace ground equipment (AGE) mechanic, military training instructor (MTI), aircraft maintenance leader, first sergeant, command first sergeant, and eventually command chief at the largest joint base in the Department of Defense.

When I enlisted, there was a push to get more women into maintenance roles. I was one of those women, thanks to my job selection indifference and high electrical and mechanical aptitude scores. At my first duty station, I was one of only two women in a shop of about ninety men. I quickly learned to armor up. No vulnerability. No softness. Just grit, toughness, endurance, and silence.

My sponsor—the only other woman in the shop—had warned me to be ready before I even set foot on the military installation. She picked me up at the airport and spent the ride back giving me an orientation of sorts. She advised me directly and clearly: Once the guys found out I was married, they'd treat me badly or at best, ignore me. She had been accepted as "one of the guys." She was exceptionally tall, strong, and had grown up working on farm equipment. I was five feet two with no similar background. I knew I had no chance of being accepted the same way, especially after what she'd just told me. So I worked harder, stayed quieter, and built my identity around being the toughest, dirtiest, grittiest mechanic in the room.

It took ten years before someone gave me permission to think I might be doing it wrong.

At the time, I was an MTI, still fairly new to the role. There weren't many women in the field, but more than I'd seen in AGE. Most of them were tough, hard-edged—just like I thought I had to be. Then one of my fellow women MTIs said something that stuck with me forever: "You can be tough and feminine. Being a woman doesn't make me weak."

That one comment shifted something. I started wearing makeup to work—not because I had to, but because I wanted to. I got my nails done. I stopped fearing looking feminine. But it would still take years to unlearn the idea that asking for help was weakness. That showing my human side was a liability. That vulnerability was something to hide.

I wish I'd had my wing-sister at my side to help me learn to lean on others, and to affirm that acting like a human was not something to be avoided at all costs. Wearing a mask for so long was exhausting, and it took a long time to even figure out what was underneath it. Peeling it off—bit by bit—has been one of the most liberating experiences of my life.

That's why this book matters. That's why you need its message.

In *SOFT: Stoically Optimistic Females Triumph*, Dr. Chaunté Hall offers a philosophy and a movement for anyone who has ever been told they had to be either strong or soft, never both. She shows us how our weirdness, our empathy, our trauma, and our tenderness are part of our power, not proof of weakness. She gives voice to what many of us have felt but never said aloud.

The stories she shares and the philosophy behind this book can help you come to terms with accepting all of you as valuable, powerful, and stronger than you know. Reading this, I realized that as far as I have come, there's always more room to grow, and I'm certainly not done. *SOFT* doesn't mean fragile. It means fierce in a new way—rooted, resilient, and real. And that's beautiful.

Because growth doesn't end. And strength doesn't have to shout.

The world doesn't need more perfection—it needs more people willing to be real. That's why this book couldn't have come at a better time.

You have power and more strength than you realize, and this book will help you connect to the *SOFT* part of your soul that can withstand every storm.

—Casy D. Boomershine,
Chief Master Sergeant (Retired)

SOFT—A Movement,
Not a Mindset

BEFORE I EVER wore the uniform or stood in front of a room leading others, the *SOFT* movement was already alive in me, because it was alive in my home.

Both of my parents served in the United States Air Force. They were disciplined, devoted, and resilient. But it wasn't just their service that shaped me, it was the way they chose to live that service out loud. My mother made the decision to step away from her military career to raise my brothers and me while supporting my father's professional path. It was not a sacrifice born of weakness, but rather a choice rooted in purpose, strength, and faith. She led our home with quiet confidence, patience, and grace, showing me that being present and nurturing wasn't small work—it was soul work.

My father, a strong and steady leader, often found himself facing women in the workplace who tried to match or exceed his authority by acting more traditionally masculine, thinking it was the only way to rise in the organizational hierarchy. But instead of being threatened, he stood his ground with calm, respectful strength. He showed me that true leadership doesn't require power plays—it requires character.

Together, my parents instilled a set of values that mirrored the *SOFT* philosophy long before I ever put a name to it: Keep your faith first. Lead with love. And never forget that your feminine energy is a gift, not something to mute, minimize, or defend.

That foundation is why, years later, I didn't break when a senior-ranking woman in the Air Force pulled me aside and said, "You're too nice. Too *SOFT*. You need to be firmer and look tougher." I remember standing there, stunned by her comment, thinking, *I am tough. I just don't feel the need to look miserable to prove it.* I did more push-ups than most. I had the discipline, the leadership skills, and a coveted list of credentials. But I also had kindness, warmth, and empathy, and I wasn't going to silence those character traits in order to look more "in charge."

That moment stuck with me because it reflected a broader problem: the world's assumption that strength must be aggressive; that power must come with a hardened edge. But I knew better. I had been raised to know better. I didn't need to become someone else to be respected. I needed to become more of who I already was.

That choice to live fully and fearlessly as myself is what led me here.

Welcome to *SOFT*: Stoically Optimistic Females Triumph

THE ACRONYM SAYS it all. *SOFT* is about reclaiming the beauty and power in qualities too often dismissed: optimism, resilience, vulnerability, and grace under pressure. It's for the woman who refuses to fit neatly into one stereotype—the woman who chooses not to compromise her warmth for the sake of appearing stronger.

SOFT is more than a clever acronym or a philosophy, it's a movement. A radical, life-affirming call to stop hardening ourselves for the comfort of others. It's about stepping fully into our *SOFTness* and understanding that our greatest strength lies in our humanity. In our care. In our faith. In our ability to lead with empathy and endure adversity with hope.

This movement is deeply personal. I've lived the tension between being strong for others while craving permission to be *SOFT* for myself. As a mother, a professional, and a leader, I've often carried the weight of doing it all, without ever letting the *SOFTness* show. But redefining what it means to be strong gave me freedom, clarity, and peace.

SOFT isn't about creating another self-improvement checklist. It's about making a cultural shift. It's about rising together to live boldly, love deeply, and lead authentically.

So, if you're ready to embrace your *SOFT* side—without apologies, excuses, or the pressure to conform—then let's begin. This book isn't a manual. It's a conversation with your most authentic self. It's a reminder that, yes, you can be stoic and optimistic, strong and *SOFT*, all at once.

Let's start this movement together with faith, courage, and maybe a bit of laughter along the way.

CHAPTER ONE

THE POWER OF AWKWARDNESS

LET'S BE HONEST—AWKWARDNESS happens. Whether you're at a work meeting, a social gathering, or even just running errands, there are times when you can't escape feeling a bit out of place. It's especially true when you're a woman who doesn't fit neatly into the boxes society has prepared for you. But here's the secret: Awkwardness isn't just a random experience. It's directly linked to your self-awareness and your "positionality" as related to pre-established societal norms.

Positionality refers to the way your identity, background, and experiences shape how you interact with the world around you, and how the world in turn interacts with you. For women, particularly those of us who embrace independence, confidence, and authenticity, our mere presence can create situations where we feel "out of place" or awkward. But what if I told you that this awkwardness is not a flaw, but a form of power? It's a reflection of the spaces we occupy, challenging traditional norms and forcing the world to reckon with our presence. And, when we embrace it, we turn that awkwardness into strength.

Imagine you're at a professional event, discussing your work, when someone—likely with the best intentions—interrupts to compliment your outfit instead of engaging with your ideas. Suddenly, the energy shifts. That familiar twinge of awkwardness hits you, not because you did anything wrong, but because at that moment you're being seen more for your appearance than your intellect. It's a jarring reminder of the subtle biases that still linger, especially for women in spaces where they've had to work twice as hard to be heard. But here's the thing: That interaction, uncomfortable as it is, reveals your strength. You're challenging norms just by showing up fully and authentically, and that is exactly where your power lies.

When you embrace your *SOFT* side, you stop seeing these moments as uncomfortable missteps and start seeing them as opportunities to reshape how others see you, and, more importantly, how you see yourself. Awkwardness isn't a sign that you don't belong; it's a sign that your presence is reshaping the conversation.

In societies that often expect women to conform, our *SOFT* side empowers us and enables us to navigate spaces that weren't initially designed with women in mind. That's where awkwardness comes in. It's a byproduct of growth, of stepping into roles and spaces that challenge stereotypes and push boundaries. And when you lean into that discomfort, it becomes your tool for change. Instead of recoiling from these moments, you can use them as a reminder that your presence, your voice, and your perspective are valuable.

Our positionality affects not only professional spaces, but it also plays out in every facet of our lives. Think about family gatherings or social events where you find yourself explaining your career choices, relationship status, or lifestyle to those who don't quite get it.

Again, the awkwardness emerges, a reflection of how your identity and choices clash with others' expectations. But here's the empowering truth: Such moments are actually a sign that you are living authentically, despite the discomfort and the risk of being misunderstood. It's

THE POWER OF AWKWARDNESS

your *SOFTness* coming into full view and showing others that there's more than one way to exist in the world.

True self-awareness shapes these interactions and allows a shift in perspective to see them as opportunities rather than pitfalls. Let's explore how recognizing and embracing your *SOFT* side can transform uneasy moments—whether in professional settings, personal relationships, or everyday interactions—into powerful opportunities for growth and empowerment.

More than just a fleeting feeling, positionality is a reflection of the tension between your true self and the roles society expects you to play. It's a reminder that you are occupying spaces where you stand out, and that's a good thing. Your true power lies in discovering who you are despite the challenging stereotypes and others' neat little cages. So, the next time you feel awkward, remember it's not a flaw, it's a sign of growth. You are owning who you are, and that's where your true strength resides.

Let's embrace the awkwardness. Let's thrive in it. Let's own who we are with pride, knowing that every uncomfortable moment is a step toward reshaping the world around us on our own terms.

An Awkward Opportunity

One of my most memorably "awkward" moments taught me more about strength than any polished, "perfect" interaction ever could. I had been invited to speak at a professional event, a big-deal conference where industry leaders were gathering to share ideas. I had prepared my presentation meticulously, running through it over and over in my head. I walked on stage feeling a mix of excitement and nervousness, ready to share my insights with an attentive audience.

And then the unthinkable happened.

Less than a minute into my talk, the projector failed. The slides I had worked so hard to perfect went black, leaving me standing there with nothing but a microphone and a room full of expectant faces. I froze. My heart raced as I tried to figure out what to do. Should I apologize profusely? Wait awkwardly for the tech team to fix it? Scrap my talk entirely?

The silence stretched out, and I could feel the weight of all those eyes on me. I felt completely exposed and vulnerable in the most awkward way possible.

But then something clicked. That moment wasn't about the slides. It wasn't about delivering a flawless presentation. It was about connecting with the audience, sharing my perspective, and showing up as my authentic self. I took a deep breath, smiled, and said, "Well, it seems technology isn't a fan of my talk today. Let's see if we can win it over."

The audience chuckled. That chuckle was my opening. I acknowledged the situation—including my awkwardness and their discomfort—and shifted gears. Instead of relying on slides, I started telling the story behind my presentation, focusing on the heart of my message rather than the visuals. I made eye contact, asked questions, and leaned into the humanity of the situation.

By the time the projector finally came back to life, we were all laughing. My talk wasn't perfect, but it was real, and in that vulnerability I found connection. I finished my presentation feeling more empowered than I ever had at a podium. The questions afterward were lively and engaging, and a colleague later told me, "That was one of the most authentic talks I've ever seen. It felt like you were really talking to us, not at us."

That experience taught me a lesson I've carried ever since: Awkwardness is not a sign of failure, it's an opportunity. In that moment of imperfection, I had the chance to be real, to connect, and to show that I didn't have to have it all together to make an impact.

Similar situations have happened to so many of us. So, let's take it a step further. Understanding your positionality can provide insight into why certain situations make you feel uncomfortable, awkward, or out of place. And more importantly, that understanding reveals how you can use your awareness to navigate those interactions with confidence and grace.

I've created a Positionality Assessment to help you identify the aspects of your identity and experiences that may influence when, where, and why you feel awkward. By reflecting on these questions, you'll not only understand yourself better but also gain clarity on how your unique position in the world is an asset, even in moments of discomfort.

POSITIONALITY ASSESSMENT

Take some time to reflect on the following questions. Feel free to journal your responses or simply sit with them in quiet contemplation. The goal is to explore the factors that shape your interactions with the world and to pinpoint the spaces where you might feel awkward because of your positionality.

1. *Who am I?*
   - What aspects of your identity shape how you experience the world? Think about your gender, race, ethnicity, age, education, socioeconomic background, and other factors that contribute to how you move through different situations.
   - How have these aspects of your identity influenced the way others perceive you?

2. *When do I experience awkwardness?*
   - Are there specific times when you feel awkward or uncomfortable? This could be during public speaking, when asserting yourself, or when you're the only one in the room with a particular perspective.

+ Is there a pattern? For example, do you feel this way more in professional settings, social gatherings, or when dealing with authority figures?

3. *Why do I feel awkward?*
   + Think about the deeper reasons behind your discomfort. Is it because you feel you don't fit the expected mold in certain spaces? Is it because your opinions, values, or experiences differ from the norm?
   + How does your positionality—the unique combination of your identity, experiences, and background—contribute to these feelings?

4. *How do I typically respond to awkwardness?*
   + When you feel awkward, how do you react? Do you become quiet, overly accommodating, defensive, or anxious?
   + How would you like to respond differently in the future? What would it look like for you to embrace the awkwardness and turn it into an empowering experience?

5. *Where does my power come from, and how can I use it with intention?*
   + Reflect on the environments where your lived experience, identity, or insight grants you influence. Are there spaces where your perspective is not only needed but powerful, even if it disrupts the status quo?
   + How can you leverage your experiences and identity to uplift others, challenge outdated systems, or drive meaningful change?

THE *SOFT* WAY FORWARD

This assessment is important not only to help you understand why you feel awkward but also to help you reframe those interactions.

So, the next time you walk into a room and feel that familiar twinge of awkwardness, remember this: It's not a sign that you don't belong. It's a sign you're bringing something new and valuable to the table. You're expanding the boundaries of that space with your unique presence. And that, my friend, is power.

With this awareness of your positionality, you can move forward in life with a deeper understanding of why certain moments feel awkward and how to navigate them with grace and strength. More than simply surviving the awkwardness, you'll be thriving in it.

This is what it means to embody the spirit of *SOFT*: *Stoically Optimistic Females Triumph.* It's about standing tall in your own skin, turning times of discomfort into opportunities for growth, and owning your space with confidence, knowing that your *SOFTness* is your strength.

CHAPTER TWO

REDEFINING STRENGTH, THE *SOFT* WAY

S TRENGTH HAS BEEN defined for us repeatedly by society, by media, and by history. We're told that strength is toughness, resilience, and the ability to push through adversity without flinching. We're taught that strength is something hard, unyielding, and often detached. But what if I told you that strength doesn't always have to be defined by how rigid you can be in the face of difficulty? What if strength could be *SOFT*?

This is where the concept of *SOFT: Stoically Optimistic Females Triumph* comes into play. It's about redefining strength on our terms, as women who are both optimistic and resilient, *SOFT* and powerful. It's time to shift the narrative and expand what strength looks like, especially for women who are told to harden themselves to fit into a world that often misunderstands their power.

The Traditional View of Strength

The traditional view of strength is built on a model of toughness. You've probably heard it before: "Don't show your emotions," "Don't let them see you sweat," "Push through the pain." We see it in the way women are encouraged to prove themselves in male-dominated industries, in leadership roles, and even in personal relationships. We're taught that to succeed, we must be resilient, unemotional, and self-sufficient, no matter the cost.

While resilience and determination are important aspects of strength, they aren't the whole story. Too often, this version of strength leaves little room for the full spectrum of who we are—our *SOFTness*, our empathy, our ability to nurture, and our capacity to care deeply. These qualities are frequently dismissed as weaknesses, yet they are some of the most powerful tools we possess.

The *SOFT* way asks us to redefine what it means to be strong, not by rejecting resilience, but by broadening it to include *SOFTness* and optimism. It's about understanding that real strength isn't just about how much you can endure. Real strength is about how gracefully you adapt, how open you remain to hope and possibility, and how deeply you care for yourself and others in the process.

The Strength in *SOFT*ness

Let's take a closer look at *SOFTness*. In a world that equates power with force, *SOFTness* is often viewed as a vulnerability. But here's the truth: There is incredible strength in *SOFTness*. It's the kind of strength that doesn't need to overpower others to make its presence known. It's the quiet, steady force that keeps you grounded in your values, even when the world is spinning out of control.

Think about water. It's *SOFT*, fluid, and adaptable, yet it's one of the most powerful forces on earth. It carves out canyons, smooths rough stones, and sustains life. The same is true of us when we embrace the strength of our own *SOFTness*. Being *SOFT* doesn't mean being weak. It means being flexible, compassionate, and open. It means having the courage to stay true to yourself, even when the world tells you to be otherwise.

Being *SOFT* means you don't have to suppress your emotions to be taken seriously. It means you can lead with empathy, set boundaries with kindness, and stay optimistic even in the face of challenges. This kind of strength isn't about pushing through at all costs. It's about knowing when to pause, when to rest, and when to ask for help. It's requires allowing yourself to be vulnerable, knowing that vulnerability is not a weakness but rather a doorway to deeper connection and growth.

Letting Go of Perfection

A crucial part of redefining strength is letting go of the idea that you must be perfect to be powerful. Perfectionism often masquerades as strength, but in reality, it's a form of self-imposed rigidity that prevents you from fully embracing who you are. Real strength lies in embracing your imperfections and learning from them.

Being *SOFT* means accepting that you don't have to have it all figured out to be worthy of respect, success, or love. Strength isn't about never making mistakes. It's about how you pick yourself up afterward, how you learn and grow, and how you treat yourself with compassion along the way.

Several years ago, I found myself in what I thought would be a routine leadership meeting. While managing a team working on a high-stakes project, tensions ran high due to tight deadlines. As the leader, I felt the burden to hold everything together, to be the unyielding pillar of strength everyone could rely on.

Midway through the meeting, one of my team members spoke up with frustration. "I just don't see how this is going to work. We're all stretched too thin, and no one seems to be listening to the challenges we're facing."

The room fell silent. You could almost hear the seriousness of those words settling into the space between us. I could feel the eyes of the team on me—some anxious, some expectant, some exhausted. The air felt thick, like we were all holding our breath, waiting for a release.

That familiar tightening in my chest began—the pressure to perform, to fix everything, to have the perfect answer ready. A younger version of me might have jumped in immediately, trying to calm the tension with a rapid solution or a rehearsed pep talk. But instead, I paused. I let the silence linger just long enough to gather my thoughts and ground myself. Because this wasn't just about solving a logistical problem, it was about acknowledging the real fatigue and frustration in the room and responding with clarity, connection, and grace.

That's where leadership lives—in the space between pressure and presence. It was at that moment I realized my team didn't need another layer of rigid control. They needed me to listen, to empathize, and to acknowledge the struggles. They needed me to be *SOFT*.

Taking a deep breath, I set my notes aside and spoke with honesty. "You're right, this isn't easy, and I know some of us are feeling overwhelmed. I don't have all the answers right now, but what I do know is that we're in this together. Let's step back and talk about what's really going on: what's working, what's not, and how we can support each other better."

It wasn't a polished response. I didn't come across as the infallible leader who always had everything under control. But what happened next was transformative. One by one, my team members began sharing their challenges, frustrations, and ideas. The tone of the conversation shifted from tension to collaboration. By the end of the meeting, we had a clearer path forward and, more importantly, a renewed sense of trust and connection.

The outcome of that meeting taught me an invaluable lesson: Real strength is not pretending to have it all figured out. It's showing up authentically, even when you feel uncertain. My willingness to embrace SOFTness—to listen, to empathize, and to admit my own limitations—didn't diminish my leadership. It strengthened it. The power wasn't in asserting control but in creating space for vulnerability, collaboration, and shared growth.

This is what it means to redefine strength in the *SOFT* way. Empathy and vulnerability are not signs of weakness; they're signs of courage. By stepping away from the traditional, rigid model of strength, we create deeper connections with those around us and open the door to more meaningful and impactful solutions.

REDEFINING STRENGTH IN PRACTICE

So, how do we begin to redefine strength in our everyday lives? It starts with embracing the idea that strength isn't just about enduring, it's about flourishing. It's about honoring the fullness of who you are—your *SOFT* edges, your optimism, your emotional depth—as sources of power.

Here are a few ideas to help you start redefining strength in your life the *SOFT* way:

1. *Lead with Empathy:* Whether you're in a leadership position at work, in your family, or in your community, remember that empathy is a form of strength. Listening deeply to others, understanding their needs, and responding with compassion are not only powerful communication methods, but also ways to build trust and stronger connections.

2. *Set Boundaries with Kindness:* Setting boundaries isn't about shutting people out. It's about protecting your energy and well-being.

You can say no without feeling guilty, and you can set limits with love. When you protect your space, you create room for what truly matters, and that's an act of self-respect and strength.

3. *Embrace Vulnerability:* Vulnerability is not the opposite of strength—it's a critical part of it. Being open about your struggles, fears, and needs requires courage. It also allows others to see the real you, fostering more authentic and supportive relationships.

4. *Practice Optimism:* Optimism is often misunderstood as naive or unrealistic, but true optimism is grounded in resilience. It's the belief that even in the face of difficulty, there's potential for growth and possibility. Staying hopeful, even when things are tough, is one of the strongest things you can do for yourself and those around you.

5. *Adapt with Grace:* Life will throw curveballs, and part of being strong is knowing how to adapt when things don't go according to plan. Instead of resisting change or pushing through at all costs, allow yourself to be flexible. Trust that you can manage whatever comes your way, and approach challenges with a sense of openness and curiosity.

The SOFT Way Forward

The next time you find yourself in a situation where strength is expected, ask yourself: What kind of strength is needed here? Is it the unyielding kind that shuts out emotion, or is it the quiet, steady kind that leans into compassion, collaboration, and authenticity? In choosing the latter, you embody the SOFT way—proving that SOFTness is not only powerful but also transformative.

As we redefine strength together, I want you to remember that your SOFTness, your optimism, and your empathy are not barriers to success; they are the keys to it. You don't have to harden yourself to be strong. You don't have to reject your emotions to be powerful. You don't have to sacrifice your well-being to prove your worth.

You can be SOFT and strong. You can be optimistic and resilient. You can triumph, not despite your SOFTness, but because of it.

The SOFT way embraces a new definition of strength—one that honors your full humanity and empowers you to move through the world with confidence, grace, and compassion. It's about knowing that real power isn't found in force or control, but in the ability to stay true to yourself no matter what.

As we move forward in this journey together, remember you are strong, not because you push through without feeling, but because you allow yourself to feel and still keep moving. That is the true strength of being *SOFT,* and that's where your power lies.

CHAPTER THREE

How to Rise Above the Stereotype Struggle

W E'VE ALL ENCOUNTERED those invisible yet pervasive boxes that society tries to put us in. Whether you've been labeled "the strong independent woman," "the emotional one," or "the quiet one," stereotypes have a way of invading every corner of our lives. They follow us into the workplace, our personal relationships, and even our inner thoughts, dictating how we're perceived and, sometimes, how we see ourselves.

Stereotypes are tricky. On the surface, they may seem harmless or even flattering. "Strong independent woman" sounds empowering, right? But dig a little deeper, and you'll find that stereotypes, even the seemingly positive ones, limit us. They reduce the complexity of who we are to a single narrative that often oversimplifies our experiences and expectations.

The real challenge isn't just in recognizing these stereotypes but in rising above them, embracing the fullness of our identities, and defining ourselves on our own terms. This includes tackling the societal labels that try to define us and finding the courage to challenge them. It's important to understand how stereotypes shape our positionality in the world and how we can break free from them in order to live more authentically.

In *SOFT: Stoically Optimistic Females Triumph*, we do this by embracing our full humanity—our *SOFTness*, strength, and everything in between—and refusing to be reduced to a single, oversimplified story.

The Weight of Stereotypes

Stereotypes can feel like invisible chains, subtly (or not so subtly) constraining our behavior, decisions, and even our aspirations. As women, we are often navigating multiple, conflicting societal expectations: Be strong, but not too strong; be nurturing, but not too emotional; be successful, but not intimidating. These expectations are not just exhausting, they're impossible to fulfill. And yet, we often find ourselves contorting into these prescribed molds, trying to fit into a world that doesn't fully see us as we are.

One of the most common stereotypes many of us face is the "strong independent woman." On the surface, it sounds like something we should aspire to, because strength and independence are often viewed as positive traits. But this stereotype comes with hidden expectations. If you're "strong and independent," you're not allowed to ask for help. You're expected to carry the weight of the world on your shoulders without complaint. Vulnerability, emotional expression, or the need for support are seen as contradictions to this label.

Similarly, the stereotype of being "emotional" often carries negative connotations. Women, in particular, are frequently labeled as overly emotional or too sensitive, as if having emotions is a weakness.

But let's flip the narrative. Emotions are a powerful source of insight, empathy, and connection. Being in touch with your emotions—and expressing them—doesn't make you weak, it makes you human. It makes you capable of building deeper relationships, fostering understanding, and navigating the complexities of life with resilience.

Stereotypes try to shrink us, to make us fit into society's narrow definition of who we should be. However, you are far too multifaceted, too layered, and too complex to be contained by a single label. The real power comes in recognizing these stereotypes for the limiting constructs they are and deciding to reject them.

Why Stereotypes Persist

Stereotypes endure because they offer a simplistic way for society to categorize and understand people. They provide a shorthand for expectations that is often based on outdated or misguided beliefs about gender, age, socioeconomic status, or any number of identity markers. But just because something is easy doesn't mean it's right. In fact, stereotypes often do more harm than good, especially for women navigating a world entrenched in rigid social norms.

Our positionality often determines which stereotypes are applied to us. For instance, a woman from one economic background may face different stereotypes than a woman from another. Stereotypes can also be linked to professions, education levels, or even regional differences. What stereotypes have in common is that they are often a reflection of society's discomfort with complexity and authenticity, seeking to simplify what cannot be easily understood or controlled.

But stereotypes persist not because they are true, but because they go unchallenged. They thrive in the absence of pushback, feeding on silence and compliance. The more we accept these labels without questioning them, the more power they hold over us. That's why rising above them isn't just an act of defiance, it's an act of liberation.

During my transition from the Air Force to the civilian sector, I found myself navigating an entirely new set of expectations and stereotypes.

As a veteran, particularly one with multiple deployments, people often assumed I would embody a very specific kind of strength—emotionless, unflinching, and hyper-competent. I was proud of my military service and the resilience it built in me. But I was also striving to bring a broader set of qualities into this new phase of my life: curiosity, empathy, and the capacity for reflection.

In a room full of senior professionals presenting ideas for a leadership development program, I decided to speak out about the importance of fostering inclusion and emotional intelligence in the workplace. I could feel the resistance before anyone said a word—tight-lipped smiles, furtive glances, the kind of silence that speaks volumes. Then one of the men finally said what others were likely thinking: "You must be great under pressure with your military background, but I'm not sure how this *SOFTer* stuff applies to leadership."

The familiar burden of a stereotype pressed down on me; the "tough-as-nails veteran" who thrived in chaos but might struggle with nuance or emotional intelligence. I could have leaned into that label, allowing myself to be reduced to the hardness they expected, and pivoted to a more "practical" topic. However, that wasn't the story I wanted to tell about myself. My experiences in the Air Force had taught me to adapt and to lead with empathy. I knew that human connection is as vital in decision-making as tactical precision. Those qualities were as much a part of my identity as my deployments or my doctorate.

So, I leaned in and let them know I truly appreciated the perspective. Then I shared what many people often miss: My military background didn't just teach me how to make tough decisions under pressure. It taught me that the most effective leaders—the ones people trusted and followed—were not only decisive, but they were also empathetic. They knew their teams. They listened, even in the most high-stakes moments.

That trust, that connection, wasn't a "nice-to-have" element—it was essential. That's why what some dismiss as "*SOFTer* stuff" isn't optional in leadership. It's the difference between people following because they're told to and people following because they believe in you.

The room went quiet for a moment. Then one of the participants nodded and said, "I hadn't thought of it that way before." That shift from skepticism to understanding was a reminder of the power in rejecting stereotypes and claiming the full scope of who we are.

Confronting Stereotypes

Rising above societal stereotypes doesn't mean pretending they don't exist. It means confronting them head-on and choosing to define yourself outside of the narrow boundaries they impose. It means taking control of your narrative and living in a way that reflects your true self, not the version of you others expect.

Stereotypes often arise from society's discomfort with complexity. My identity as a veteran, a single mother, a business professional, and yes, as "Dr. Hall," rarely fits neatly into one box. That tension creates the perfect breeding ground for oversimplified assumptions about who I am and how I got here.

I remember being introduced at an event as Dr. Hall. Although it is an honorific I earned through years of late nights, discipline, and relentless focus, I could immediately see the shift in how I was perceived. A few people stiffened. Their smiles became tighter. One even commented later, half-jokingly, "Well, it must be nice to come from that kind of privilege."

That moment stopped me cold. Because nothing about my journey was handed to me. I didn't grow up with academic or financial privileges. I enlisted in the Air Force at seventeen. I worked for everything I have. Every classroom I stepped into, every degree I earned, was possible because I said yes to opportunity, yes to growth, yes to support, and yes to believing I belonged, even when others doubted it.

I smiled and responded with warmth but also with clarity. I shared that my education came by way of military service, sacrifice, and seizing every chance to learn and lead. I wasn't just standing in that room as Dr. Hall because of titles. I was there because I knew how to show up—*SOFT* when it called for grace, strong when it called for grit.

That experience reminded me again that I don't have to choose between parts of myself. I can be both the strategic, decisive leader shaped by my deployments *and* the empathetic, reflective woman who values connection and growth. I can be someone who earned her degrees with discipline and service *and* someone who still feels that pang when her background is reduced to a label.

This is the heart of rising above stereotypes: refusing to let society's narrow definitions limit the full expression of who you are. Instead of bending under labels and assumptions, you reclaim your story— demonstrating the depth, complexity, and strength that comes from living all of who you are. And when you do that, you don't just rise, you lead. On your terms. In your truth.

Rising Above Societal Labels and Stereotypes

Here are some suggestions to help you identify, redefine, and transcend stereotypes in your life the *SOFT* way:

1. *Acknowledge and Reflect:* The first step to rising above stereotypes is to acknowledge when they're affecting you. Ask yourself: What labels do I feel pressured to live up to? How do these stereotypes shape my decisions or the way I interact with others? Recognizing the influence of societal labels is key to beginning to break free from them.

2. *Redefine Strength and Vulnerability:* In *SOFT: Stoically Optimistic Females Triumph*, we redefine strength to include *SOFTness*, empathy, and vulnerability. You don't have to be indifferent and unfeeling to be strong. In fact, true strength comes from being able to show up as your full self, emotions and all. Challenge the idea that vulnerability is a weakness by noticing the moments where your vulnerability actually creates more connection, more impact, and more personal power. Then embrace that openness as a vital part of your strength.

3. *Tell Your Own Story:* Stereotypes are society's attempt to write your story for you. But you are the author of your own narrative. Take control of the story you want to tell. When you feel the pressure of societal labels, remind yourself: I am more than a stereotype. I am the sum of my experiences, my values, and my choices.

4. *Show Up Authentically:* One of the most powerful ways to rise above stereotypes is to live authentically. This means showing up as your full, complex self, even when it feels uncomfortable or when others don't know how to respond. The more you embrace your authenticity, the less power stereotypes have over you. You are not confined to a single label or expectation. You are a whole, dynamic individual.

5. *Embrace Your Multiplicity:* Women are not one-dimensional. We can be strong and *SOFT*, independent and nurturing, logical and emotional. Embrace the multiplicity of who you are and resist the urge to shrink yourself to fit societal molds. You are allowed to be complex, layered, and full of contradictions. In fact, that's where your true power lies.

THE *SOFT* WAY FORWARD

In *SOFT*, we redefine what it means to be strong by embracing the full spectrum of our humanity. We recognize that the labels society tries to impose on us—whether they involve strength, vulnerability, independence, or emotions—are incomplete. And we refuse to let those labels define us.

The next time you feel the heaviness of a stereotype pressing down on you, take a moment to pause. Remember that you are not bound by society's expectations. You have the power to rise above those labels, to live authentically, and to define strength on your own terms.

Because in the end, being *SOFT* is more than just surviving societal labels. It's thriving despite them. It's showing up as your whole, authentic self, embracing your complexity, and reclaiming your power. And when you do that, the stereotypes that once held you back will have no choice but to fade away.

CHAPTER FOUR

Grace Under Pressure— The Art of Stoic Optimism

YOU KNOW HOW it feels when life seems to be falling apart. When work deadlines pile up, family obligations mount, and personal challenges seem to hit all at once. Chaos is inevitable, but how you respond to it is what sets you apart.

In those moments of pressure, staying calm may feel impossible, but that's where Stoic Optimism comes in. It's the art of remaining grounded and composed even when the world feels like it's spinning out of control. This is the *SOFT* way of handling turmoil with grace, clarity, and quiet strength.

At its core, Stoic Optimism is a balance between accepting life's difficulties while still holding on to hope. It's about understanding that while we can't control everything that happens, we can always control how we react. It's choosing to see challenges as opportunities for growth rather than as setbacks. This mindset doesn't settle for simply enduring hardship, it allows us to thrive through it.

What Is Stoic Optimism?

To understand Stoic Optimism, it helps to break the term down. The philosophy of Stoicism, which has been around for centuries, teaches that we cannot control external events, but only our responses to them. It emphasizes resilience, self-control, and understanding that our thoughts shape our reality. Stoicism doesn't ask us to suppress emotions, but rather to focus on what we can control and let go of what we can't.

Optimism, on the other hand, is the belief that things can and will get better, even in the face of difficulty. It's about maintaining hope, seeing potential solutions, and recognizing that challenges are often temporary. While optimism can sometimes be misunderstood as naive, true optimism is grounded in realism. It's the strength to see the silver lining without denying the storm.

When we combine stoicism and optimism, we get a powerful approach to life: Stoic Optimism. It's the ability to stay calm in the face of negative circumstances, to acknowledge our emotions without being overwhelmed by them, and to remain hopeful, even when the path forward is unclear. In *SOFT*, this philosophy becomes the foundation of our strength. It allows us to remain poised, confident, and in control of our own narratives, no matter what life throws our way.

Grace Under Pressure

Grace is often described as elegance in movement, but grace under pressure is moving through life's challenges with poise, dignity, and self-awareness. It isn't pretending everything is fine, but responding to difficulties with a calm and steady presence. It's finding that quiet inner strength when everything else feels overwhelming.

When you are under pressure, whether it's a major life transition, a stressful work situation, or an unexpected crisis, grace means acknowledging the chaos without letting it consume you. It's taking a deep breath, assessing the situation, and choosing a measured response rather than reacting impulsively. Grace is knowing when to act and when to let go. It's the ability to hold space for both your emotions and your logic, allowing them to coexist without conflict.

Less than twenty-four hours after receiving the call from my supervisor, I learned that my unplanned, unexpected deployment orders had come through—this time with the Army. As an Air Force veteran with two deployments behind me, I wasn't new to operational challenges, but this was uncharted territory. I had never deployed alongside my Army brothers and sisters before, and our team was immediately tasked with completing a rigorous thirty-day training cycle to prepare for the mission.

The training was grueling—long days of learning Army-specific protocols, adjusting to their culture, and mastering tactical skills outside my usual Air Force scope. Just as I found my rhythm and began mentally preparing for our combat lifesaver mission, another curveball was thrown our way. Upon arrival, our mission changed abruptly. Most of the team was forward deployed to another camp, while a few of us stayed behind to close up operations at our staging base.

The isolation hit hard. I'd gone from being part of a tightly knit unit to living in a tent solo and managing an entire operation with two men. There was no roadmap for this situation. As we packed up sensitive equipment, coordinated logistics with little to no support, and maintained morale, I battled the emotional weight of feeling isolated, disconnected, and scared.

At first, I felt overwhelmed. It was the kind of blunt force that hits you in the chest—tightening, disorienting, and heavy. This wasn't what I had trained for. After weeks of mentally and physically preparing for a critical mission, I found myself sidelined, tasked with cleaning up and closing out operations while the rest of the team moved on. It felt like everything I had braced for—every drill, every strategy session, every ounce of adrenaline—had evaporated into a fog of monotony and isolation. I wasn't on the front lines; I was behind, alone, in the quiet aftermath.

A flood of doubt crept in. *Why me? Had I failed? Was I not needed?* The silence around me made the questions louder.

But then, I paused. I took a deep breath, grounding myself in the stillness. I remembered something the military had taught me again and again: Focus on what you can control. That single principle became my anchor. I couldn't change the orders. I couldn't reverse the shift in mission. But I *could* control how I showed up and how I led myself, even when no one was watching.

I shifted my perspective. Instead of dwelling on the abruptly altered mission or the sense of isolation, I reframed the situation. This was still an important job, one that demanded organization, precision, and resilience.

I created a checklist, dividing the tasks into manageable parts, and set daily goals to keep myself on track. I reached out to nearby teams for coordination, building relationships that allowed me to problem-solve efficiently and feel less isolated.

I also made time to focus on self-care. In the evenings, I worked out, volunteered, and reflected on the day's accomplishments. This reminded me of the bigger picture—every action I took was ensuring that the team ahead of me had what they needed to succeed.

When the day finally came to hand over the last of the equipment and close our operation, I realized that this seemingly thankless task had been a test of grace under pressure. It wasn't about the scale of the mission. It was about showing up, staying composed, and finding purpose in the midst of chaos.

That experience taught me the essence of Stoic Optimism: finding clarity and control in the uncontrollable and holding onto hope even when the path forward seems unclear. I could have let the frustration and isolation consume me, but by reframing the situation and focusing on what I could achieve, I not only completed the mission but also grew stronger in the process.

This is what it means to embody *SOFT*: navigating challenges with grace, resilience, and a quiet confidence that says, "I can handle this." Life often throws us into situations that feel overwhelming or unfair, and in those moments you have two choices: panic or pause. Grace under pressure is choosing to pause. It's recognizing that while the situation feels out of control, *you* are still in control of your response. Instead of rushing to fix everything or becoming overwhelmed, you take a moment to assess. You calmly acknowledge the issue, find a solution, and move forward. That's the art of Stoic Optimism in action.

The Power of Resilience

At the heart of Stoic Optimism is resilience. Life will inevitably bring challenges, but resilience is the ability to bounce back, rise above adversity, and keep moving forward. Resilience doesn't mean you never feel stress or doubt. It means you trust yourself to navigate those feelings and come out stronger on the other side.

I've lived this truth in one of the most painful seasons of my life. I remember the moment I realized my ex-husband wasn't just leaving *me*—he was walking away from *our children*, too. Overnight, I became a single mother. There was no slow unraveling, no gentle warning. Just absence. And in the quiet that followed, I had a choice to make.

I didn't run to social media. I didn't publicly share the collapse of my marriage. Instead, I pressed forward. I leaned into what I *could* manage—my mindset, my children's well-being, my peace. I woke up every morning and chose to stand, even when it hurt to get out of bed. I chose to show up for my kids with love and structure. And slowly, day by day, I built a new life: one that no longer depended on someone else choosing to stay.

That's what resilience looks like. It's not loud or flashy. Sometimes it's just showing up, making breakfast, finishing the workday, and tucking your babies in at night with a heart that's still healing.

Stoic Optimism teaches us that resilience isn't about enduring hardship without breaking. It's about learning how to bend, adapt, and grow in the face of adversity. It's the quiet confidence that says, "I can figure this out," even when you don't have all the answers. And it's this mindset that allows you to move through life's chaos with grace.

PRACTICING STOIC OPTIMISM

How do you begin to cultivate Stoic Optimism in your own life? Here are a few practical steps to help you stay calm in chaos and develop grace under pressure:

1. *Focus On What You Can Control:* When life gets overwhelming, it's easy to feel like everything is slipping out of your grasp. The key to Stoic Optimism is shifting your attention to the things that *are* within your influence. You can't always control what happens, but you *can* decide how you respond. Ask yourself: What can I do right now? What's mine to manage or shift? Then channel your energy toward those choices. Clarity comes when you stop chasing what's out of reach and start acting on what's already in your hands.

2. *Pause and Breathe:* One of the most effective ways to maintain grace under pressure is to pause before reacting. When you feel stress mounting, take a moment to breathe. This simple act of slowing down allows you to clear your mind, center yourself, and make decisions from a place of peace rather than panic.

3. *Reframe the Situation:* Stoic Optimism requires seeing challenges as opportunities. When faced with chaos, ask yourself: What can I learn from this? How might this experience help me grow? Reframing difficult situations in a positive light doesn't mean ignoring the struggle, it means recognizing that there's value in every challenge.

4. *Let Go of What You Can't Control:* One of the hardest lessons in life is learning to let go. When things spiral out of control, it's natural to want to fix everything. But part of Stoic Optimism is accepting that some things are beyond your control. Letting go isn't the same thing as giving up. It's releasing the need to control outcomes and trusting that you'll be okay, no matter what happens.

5. *Stay Optimistic, Even in Uncertainty:* Optimism doesn't mean everything is perfect; it means believing in the possibility of a positive outcome. When you're in the middle of a storm, it can be hard to see the sun behind the clouds, but Stoic Optimism asks you to hold onto hope. Trust that even when things seem uncertain, there is always potential for growth, learning, and a brighter future.

6. *Be Firm Yet Kind to Yourself:* In moments of pressure, we often expect ourselves to be perfect, to handle everything with flawless precision. But grace under pressure also means being kind to yourself. Allow yourself to make mistakes, to feel stressed, or to be unsure. The key is to treat yourself with the same compassion you would offer someone else in a difficult situation.

THE *SOFT* WAY FORWARD

Grace under pressure is one of the most powerful approaches to help you embody the *SOFT* way of life. It includes staying calm, centered, and optimistic, even when things feel out of control. It's trusting yourself to manage, with poise and resilience, whatever life throws at you.

Remember, you are capable of navigating chaos with grace. You have the ability to stay grounded in the storm, to find calm in the midst of pressure, and to rise above challenges with strength and positivity. This is the art of Stoic Optimism—the ability to remain hopeful and resilient, no matter what life brings your way.

So, the next time you're faced with chaos, take a deep breath. Focus on what you can control. Let go of what you can't. And remember that within you lies the strength to handle it all with grace, optimism, and the quiet confidence of a *SOFT* woman who knows her true power.

CHAPTER FIVE

THE DANCE BETWEEN VULNERABILITY AND CONFIDENCE

V ULNERABILITY AND CONFIDENCE are two words that, at first glance, seem like polar opposites. Vulnerability is often associated with weakness, exposure, and uncertainty, while confidence suggests strength, assurance, and control. Yet, these two qualities are deeply connected, and balancing them is essential to living a fully authentic and empowered life. One does not cancel out the other. In fact, they enhance one another, creating a foundation of true self-assurance that isn't afraid of being seen, flaws and all.

In *SOFT: Stoically Optimistic Females Triumph*, we know that real strength lies in embracing both our vulnerability and our confidence, letting them dance together in harmony.

Redefining Vulnerability

Vulnerability is one of the most misunderstood traits in modern society. We're often taught that to be vulnerable is to be weak, opening ourselves up to hurt, criticism, or failure. Many of us have been conditioned to keep our guard up, to protect ourselves from potential harm by hiding our true selves behind a mask of strength. But vulnerability is not weakness. It's a form of courage that empowers us to show up fully as we are, without fear of judgment or rejection.

When we allow ourselves to be vulnerable, we let others see our true selves—our emotions, our fears, our hopes, and our imperfections. This kind of openness requires immense strength, because it involves risk. However, it's also the only way to build deep, meaningful connections. Without vulnerability, we might protect ourselves from short-term discomfort, but we also close ourselves off from the possibility of real intimacy, growth, and support.

In *SOFT*, we redefine vulnerability as a powerful tool for connection and self-discovery. It's the willingness to say, "This is who I am, with all my flaws, insecurities, and uncertainties." It's embracing the parts of ourselves we've been taught to hide, knowing that these very parts are what make us human and relatable. Vulnerability invites others to connect with us, creating a space for authentic relationships and true understanding.

Redefining Confidence

On the flip side of vulnerability is confidence: a trait that is often seen as the antidote to insecurity. Confidence is typically understood as having trust in your own abilities, decisions, and worth. It's about walking into a room with your head held high, believing in yourself regardless of external validation.

But confidence, when misunderstood, can lead to a false sense of invulnerability. We're often told that to be confident, we must always have the answers, always be in control, and never let our guard down. This type of confidence is rigid, superficial, and exhausting to maintain. It relies on external markers of success rather than an internal sense of worth.

True confidence, the kind we cultivate in *SOFT*, is not about always being in control or having it all figured out. It's about trusting yourself enough to be vulnerable. It's about knowing that your worth isn't diminished by your mistakes, insecurities, or moments of doubt. In fact, it's in those very moments, when we allow ourselves to stand tall and be seen as we truly are, that confidence is most needed.

THE VULNERABILITY AND CONFIDENCE TANGO

Vulnerability and confidence are not at odds with each other; they are partners. Confidence without vulnerability can lead to arrogance, an impenetrable shield that prevents us from truly connecting with others or learning from our experiences. Vulnerability without confidence can make us feel exposed and insecure, as though our openness is a liability rather than a strength.

But when we allow these two traits to dance together, we unlock a new kind of power. Vulnerability allows us to be real, to take risks, to show up authentically in the world. Confidence gives us the assurance that, no matter what happens, we are worthy and capable.

It was the middle of the pandemic, and like so many others, I was working from home, balancing virtual meetings, helping my kids with online school, and quietly watching the life I thought I'd built unravel behind the scenes. On the outside, nothing had changed. My video background was still neat. My credentials still sat proudly behind me on the bookshelf. I still showed up. But behind the screen, my marriage had ended, and I was navigating single motherhood in real time without a pause button or a Plan B.

During a live podcast interview, something shifted in my mind. I stumbled over my words, something I rarely did. The host gently asked, "Are you okay?" And suddenly, the armor cracked. I could've smiled and brushed it off. That would've been easy. That's what I'd always done.

Instead, I chose honesty. I told them I was going through something personal. That I was still fully committed, still showing up, but that I was also human. I didn't offer every detail, but I allowed my real self to peek through the cracks of my imperfection.

And something amazing happened. The conversation didn't fall apart. It got richer. More real. More human. My vulnerability didn't shake the room, it grounded it. People didn't see me as "less than." They saw me. And for many, it was the first time they truly *understood* who I am. Not just the professional. Not just the mom. Not just the polished bio. But the woman behind all of it.

This experience taught me that vulnerability and confidence are not opposing forces—they are soulmates. My willingness to share a glimpse of my struggles allowed me to connect with many in a deeper way, while my confidence in my ability to handle the situation ensured that I continued to lead effectively. The dance between the two recognizes that strength doesn't mean never faltering. It means showing up authentically, even when life feels messy. It involves trusting that you can handle whatever comes your way, not because you have all the answers, but because you believe in your resilience and worth.

The next time you face a personal challenge while trying to remain professional, remember this: You don't have to hide your vulnerability to be confident. By allowing both qualities to coexist, you not only honor your sense of humanity but also inspire those around you to do the same. That is the true strength of living the *SOFT* way.

CULTIVATE VULNERABILITY AND CONFIDENCE

How do we begin this dance where openness meets resolve and truth walks hand in hand with assurance? Here are a few ways to weave this powerful balance into your life:

1. *Own Your Story:* Embracing who you are means honoring every part of your journey—the highs, the heartaches, the healing. You don't need to polish your past or pretend it's perfect. Sharing the full picture, including your setbacks and flaws, isn't weakness, it's what makes you real and relatable. And when you acknowledge your growth, you reinforce your own sense of worth.

2. *Speak Up with Intention:* Telling your truth—especially when it's hard—is an act of courage. Whether you're advocating for yourself at work, expressing your needs in a relationship, or simply having an honest internal dialogue, communicating what matters builds trust in your own voice. You don't need to be loud to be heard, you just need to be genuine.

3. *Reach Out When You Need To:* There's strength in knowing when to lean on others. Despite what the world may suggest, asking for help isn't failure—it's wisdom. Letting others support you creates connection, not weakness. It says, "I value myself enough not to do it all alone."

4. *Navigate the Unknown with Faith in Yourself:* Life rarely offers complete clarity. But being grounded in who you are allows you to face uncertainty without fear. You may not always know what's next, and that's okay. What matters most is your belief that, whatever comes, you'll figure it out.

5. *Learn, Adjust, and Try Again:* Every win is worth celebrating, and every loss holds a lesson. Sometimes things fall apart. Sometimes you miss the mark. But choosing to reflect instead of retreat—and to keep showing up—is where your true power lies.

THE *SOFT* WAY FORWARD

In *SOFT*, we celebrate the full spectrum of who we are. Real strength is found when we embrace both courage and tenderness. It's about standing firmly in your worth, even when uncertainty creeps in. It's about showing up fully—even in the messiness of life—and trusting that you are enough, just as you are.

This balance doesn't demand you choose one side over the other. It happens when you allow seemingly opposite qualities to work in harmony. You can be both gentle and grounded, compassionate and bold, openhearted and self-assured, all at the same time.

As you plot your own course, remember: You don't have to dim your light or toughen your edges to be seen as capable. In fact, it's your openness that gives your strength depth. Your grace, even in vulnerability, is what makes you powerful.

Let your *SOFTness* be a source of courage and your inner belief be the compass that guides you. Together, they form the heart of what it means to live as a *SOFT* woman—authentic, empowered, and unapologetically you.

CHAPTER SIX

LEADING WITH EMPATHY— THE QUIET POWER OF CONNECTION

L EADERSHIP IS OFTEN portrayed as bold, asser-tive, and sometimes even forceful. We see leaders as those who command attention, make decisions quickly, and guide others by harnessing sheer willpower. But what if there's another way to lead? What if true leadership isn't about being the loudest or most commanding voice in the room, but rather about creating deep con-nections with others through empathy and understanding?

In *SOFT: Stoically Optimistic Females Triumph*, we believe in leading with empathy. Empathy is not only a powerful leadership tool, but it's also the key to building trust, fostering collaboration, and inspiring genuine loyalty. The quiet power of connection is often overlooked, but it's this subtle, grounded approach to leadership that can create lasting change.

This chapter explores how empathy can transform the way you lead in both your personal and professional life. Empathy recognizes that excellent leadership is not marked by exerting power over others, but by empowering those around you to thrive. Leading with empathy allows you to connect with people on a deeper level, creating an environment where everyone feels seen, heard, and valued.

What Does It Mean to Lead with Empathy?

Leading with empathy means valuing emotional intelligence as much as technical skill. It means recognizing that people are not just workers or colleagues, they are individuals with their own unique experiences, strengths, and struggles. Empathy allows us to see beyond the tasks at hand and focus on the humanity of those under our guidance.

In a leadership role, empathy shows up in many ways. It could be as simple as checking in on a team member who seems stressed, offering flexibility to someone who is juggling personal challenges, or providing encouragement when someone is struggling with self-doubt. It's about being present, listening without judgment, and responding in ways that lift others up rather than add to their burdens.

It was one of the busiest times of the year at work, and the entire team struggled under the mounting pressure of a looming high-stakes presentation. Everyone felt the strain of late nights and tight deadlines. In the midst of all this, one of my colleagues, a key contributor to the project, began missing deadlines and seemed unusually withdrawn. The easy response would have been frustration. After all, the success of the presentation depended on everyone pulling their weight. But something told me there was more to the story.

I pulled her aside after a team meeting and asked gently, "Hey, is everything okay? You don't seem like yourself lately."

Her eyes welled up with tears as she shared that she was going through a personal crisis. Her father had been hospitalized unexpectedly, and she was struggling to balance the demands of work with the emotional toll of caring for her family. She apologized profusely for falling behind, clearly worried about how it was affecting the team.

At that moment, leading with empathy became my priority. I reassured her, "I'm so sorry you're going through this. Please don't feel like you have to shoulder this alone. Let's figure out how we can support you."

We adjusted her workload, reallocating some of her responsibilities among the rest of the team. I made it clear to everyone that this wasn't a matter of picking up slack—it was showing up for a teammate in need. Over the next few weeks, I checked in regularly with her, not just about work but about how she was holding up personally. By giving her the space to focus on her family without the added weight of guilt, she was able to return to the project more energized and grateful for the team's support.

When we finally delivered the presentation, it was a success, and my colleague expressed her deep appreciation for how the team had rallied around her. "Your support made all the difference," she said. "I didn't feel judged. I felt cared for."

This experience reinforced for me the power of leading with empathy. It would have been easy to focus on the project deadlines and overlook the human element, but taking time to connect with my colleague on a personal level made all the difference. Empathy isn't about avoiding accountability or letting standards slip. It's about recognizing humanity in others and creating an environment where people feel valued and supported.

THE POWER OF CONNECTION

At the heart of empathy is connection. When we lead with empathy, we build stronger, more authentic relationships with those around us. This connection fosters trust, and trust is the foundation of any successful team or relationship.

Think about it: When was the last time you truly felt seen and heard by someone in a leadership role? How did that impact your motivation, your sense of value, or your willingness to give your best?

Now, flip it. How often do you make space to genuinely connect with those you lead or support? When people feel that their leaders care about them—not just as workers, but as individuals—they are more likely to be engaged, motivated, and loyal.

Empathy lays the groundwork for trust and transparency. When leaders demonstrate genuine care and understanding, it gives others permission to speak candidly about setbacks, needs, and even mistakes, without fear of being dismissed or judged. This openness not only makes people feel heard, but it also creates space for honest dialogue and thoughtful problem-solving.

In professional environments, empathetic leadership fuels a culture where innovation and collaboration thrive. When individuals feel truly supported, they're more willing to think creatively, voice new ideas, and take meaningful risks. They don't just show up, they lean in. Instead of bracing themselves for criticism, they engage with confidence, knowing their perspectives matter.

I've seen it firsthand. When my team knows they're safe—not just professionally, but personally—they don't just perform, they flourish. They're more loyal, more engaged, and more likely to stay. In fact, empathy not only retains great people, but it also attracts them. Because people talk about places where they feel valued. When we lead with empathy, we don't just create stronger relationships, we build a culture others want to join.

The Quiet Power of Empathy

Empathy doesn't make headlines. It's not the loudest or flashiest form of leadership, but it is one of the most powerful. Leading with empathy creates lasting impact because it touches people at a deeper level. It's not about commanding respect through authority; it's about earning trust through connection.

Leaders who prioritize empathy leave a legacy of care, compassion, and collaboration. They create environments where people feel empowered to grow, to take risks, and to be themselves. This quiet power of connection builds stronger teams, more resilient relationships, and a greater sense of community.

In *SOFT*, we understand that leadership isn't centered around being in control. *SOFT* leadership focuses on lifting others up. It recognizes the humanity in everyone you interact with and uses that awareness to guide decisions and actions. When you lead with empathy, you create space for others to thrive, and in doing so, you become a more effective, compassionate, and respected leader.

So, let me ask you: Do the people around you—at work, at home, in your community—feel safe to show up as their full selves? How might your world change if they did?

How to Lead with Empathy

Empathy is not just a buzzword in leadership, it's a powerful tool that fosters trust, deepens relationships, and builds stronger, more resilient teams. When we lead with empathy, we create environments where people feel seen, heard, and valued—not just for what they do, but for who they are. But empathy is more than a feeling; it's a practice. One we must cultivate with intention, especially in moments of stress, transition, or conflict. Consider these practical ways to incorporate empathy into your leadership style:

1. *Listen Actively:* One of the most important aspects of empathy is listening—really listening. Active listening means giving someone

your full attention without distractions or interruptions. Listen not only to the words they're saying, but also to the emotions behind those words. When you listen with empathy, you make the other person feel valued and understood.

2. *Acknowledge Emotions:* When someone is going through a tough time, don't brush it off or try to fix it immediately. Instead, acknowledge their feelings. Sometimes, simply saying, "I see you're having a hard time, and I'm here to support you," can make all the difference.

3. *Put Yourself in Their Shoes:* Ask yourself: How would I feel in this situation? What challenges might this person be facing that I'm not aware of? By putting yourself in someone else's shoes, you gain a better understanding of their needs and can respond in a more compassionate and effective way.

4. *Offer Support, Not Solutions:* When people come to us with problems, our instinct is often to jump in and offer solutions. But sometimes what they really need is support, not answers. Leading with empathy means being a source of encouragement and understanding rather than trying to fix everything. Give people the space to process their emotions and figure out the best path forward, knowing that you're there to help if they need it.

5. *Show Compassion in Difficult Conversations:* Leadership often requires having tough conversations, whether it's giving feedback, addressing conflict, or managing difficult situations. Leading with empathy doesn't mean avoiding these conversations, it means approaching them with compassion. Instead of being critical or dismissive, approach these discussions with care. Acknowledge the other person's feelings and work together to find solutions.

6. *Be Vulnerable:* Empathy is a two-way street. To truly connect with others, we must also be willing to share our own experiences and emotions. When leaders show vulnerability, they humanize themselves and create a sense of shared experience. You don't have to overshare, but be authentic about your own challenges and allow others to see that you, too, are navigating the complexities of life.

The *SOFT* Way Forward

Leadership through empathy is a core value of *SOFT*. It requires embracing a new kind of strength—one that isn't based on force or dominance, but on connection and care. As you move forward in your life, whether in formal leadership roles or with personal relationships, remember that your ability to empathize is one of your greatest strengths.

The quiet power of connection can transform the way you lead and the way you live. By choosing empathy, you create a ripple effect, inspiring others to do the same. You build stronger, more authentic relationships, foster trust and loyalty, and make a meaningful impact on the lives of those around you.

So, let's lead with empathy. Let's embrace the quiet, steady strength that comes from truly seeing and understanding others. And in doing so, let's create a world where excellent leadership isn't characterized by power, but by connection and compassion. This is the *SOFT* way, and it's the kind of leadership the world needs more than ever.

CHAPTER SEVEN

THE JOY OF SAYING NO—
SETTING BOUNDARIES
WITH COMPASSION

S AYING "NO" CAN be one of the most difficult things to do, especially for women. Whether it's a work request, a family obligation, or a social invitation, we often feel the pressure to say yes even when we're already overwhelmed. We're taught that saying yes makes us appear helpful, kind, and dependable, while saying no feels selfish, harsh, or ungrateful. But here's the truth: Saying no is one of the most empowering and compassionate things you can do, not just for yourself but for others as well.

In *SOFT: Stoically Optimistic Females Triumph*, we embrace the art of setting boundaries with compassion. Healthy boundaries are essential to maintaining balance in our lives, protecting our energy, and ensuring that we are not constantly giving away more than we have. Boundaries aren't about shutting people out; they're about creating space for what truly matters, what nourishes you, and what aligns with your values and goals.

There is joy that comes from saying no with love and kindness. It starts by understanding that boundaries are not a sign of weakness or selfishness, but a symbol of self-respect. When you set healthy boundaries, you are saying yes to yourself, your well-being, and your long-term happiness.

WHY WE STRUGGLE TO SAY NO

Saying no can feel uncomfortable for many reasons. Often, we worry about disappointing others or being perceived as unhelpful or uncaring. We might fear that saying no will damage our relationships, whether at work or in our personal lives. Many of us are taught from a young age to be accommodating, to please others, and to put our own needs last. As a result, we become conditioned to agree to everything, even when it's to our own detriment.

But constantly saying yes comes with a cost. Overcommitting leads to stress, burnout, and resentment. When we stretch ourselves too thin, we end up depleted, with little energy left for the things that truly matter. What's worse, by saying yes to things we don't really want to do, we are saying no to the things that align with our goals, values, and wellness.

The key to breaking this cycle is understanding that saying no is not a rejection. Rather, it's a choice to prioritize what's most important to you. When you set clear boundaries, you protect your time, energy, and emotional health. This allows you to be more present, engaged, and effective in the areas of your life where you choose to say yes.

With all the hats I wear—professional, volunteer, community leader—my calendar is constantly packed. I thrive on serving others and contributing to causes I believe in, but I learned early on that saying yes to everything would come at a cost. For me, the cost was time with my children, and that was a price I wasn't willing to pay. So, I made a promise to them: No matter how busy life got, I would never miss our VIP Friday nights.

VIP Friday is sacred in our household. It's a time when we order pizza, play games, and watch a movie together. No distractions, no exceptions. It's our little tradition, a space carved out just for us. And no matter how hectic the week has been, I can reconnect with my children and remind them—and myself—that they are my priority.

But that commitment hasn't always been easy to uphold. One Friday, I received a last-minute invitation to speak at a high-profile community event. The organizer emphasized how valuable my presence would be and assured me that this opportunity could open doors for future partnerships. My first instinct was to say yes. After all, it was a chance to make an impact and expand my reach for a cause I deeply cared about.

But then I thought about my children, eagerly waiting for VIP Friday. If I said yes to the event, I would be saying no to them and to the promise I had made to always protect this time. The decision was clear.

I called the organizer and thanked them for the opportunity but explained that I already had a prior commitment. "I can't make it this evening," I said, "but I'd love to explore how I can support your work in the future."

That Friday night, as we sat in the living room playing games and laughing over pizza, I felt an overwhelming sense of peace. I didn't regret declining the event invitation for a second. In that moment, I was exactly where I needed to be—fully present with my children, nurturing the bond that mattered most.

This experience taught me a powerful lesson about the importance of boundaries: Every yes is a no to something else. Saying no to that opportunity wasn't easy, but it was a compassionate choice. Compassion for myself, my children, and the values I hold dear. By setting that boundary, I protected the space for what truly matters in my life.

Boundaries are not about shutting people out; they are about creating room for the things that nourish you. In saying no with kindness and clarity, I was able to honor my priorities without guilt or hesitation. The opportunity to speak at the event was meaningful, but it wasn't more meaningful than keeping my promise to my children.

The Power of Boundaries

Boundaries are essential for maintaining healthy relationships, whether at work, with family, or in friendships. They help define what is acceptable and what is not, giving you control over your time, energy, and emotional health. When you set boundaries, you are communicating your needs, your limits, and your values to the people around you. It's an act of self-respect and an invitation for others to respect you as well.

Boundaries are not about creating distance or shutting people out. In fact, they often strengthen relationships by fostering clearer communication and mutual respect. When you set boundaries with compassion, you are teaching others how to engage with you in a healthy, respectful way.

There are numerous benefits of setting boundaries, such as:

- *Reduced Stress:* When you say no to unnecessary commitments, you free up space for the things that truly matter. This lowers stress levels and gives you the time and energy to focus on your top priorities.

- *Increased Self-Respect:* Setting boundaries sends a powerful message to yourself: I am worthy of protection and care. It reinforces the idea that your needs are valid and deserving of attention.

- *Healthier Relationships:* Boundaries help prevent resentment and burnout in relationships. When you communicate your limits with kindness, you give others the opportunity to respect your needs, leading to more balanced and mutually supportive relationships.

- *More Time for What Matters:* Every time you say yes to something that doesn't align with your goals or values, you are saying no to something that does. Setting boundaries ensures that you have more time and energy for the things that are truly important to you.

SET BOUNDARIES WITH COMPASSION

Saying no doesn't have to be harsh or confrontational. In fact, boundaries are most effective when they are set with compassion and understanding. It's possible to decline an invitation in a way that is kind, respectful, and considerate of others while still honoring your own needs. Here's how to start:

1. *Be Clear and Direct:* When setting a boundary, it's important to be clear about your limits. Avoid vague or apologetic language like, "I'm not sure I can," or "Maybe." Instead, use direct, respectful language: "I won't be able to take that on right now," or "I'm not available for this project."

2. *Avoid Over-Explaining:* You don't owe anyone a lengthy explanation for why you're saying no. Keep your response simple and to the point. Offering too much detail can invite negotiation or make you feel like you need to justify your decision. Trust that your no is enough.

3. *Acknowledge the Request:* You can say no with compassion by acknowledging the other person's request or feelings. For example, "I really appreciate you thinking of me, but I have too many commitments right now," or "I understand that this is important, but I need to prioritize my current workload."

4. *Offer an Alternative (If You Want To):* If it feels right, you can offer an alternative solution. For example, "I'm unable to help with that, but I can recommend someone who might be able to," or "I can't take on this task now, but I'd be happy to help next month."

5. *Stay Firm and Kind:* It's natural for people to push back when you set a boundary, especially if they're used to you always saying yes. Stay firm but kind. Reaffirm your no without wavering: "I understand that this is urgent, but I'm unable to take it on." You don't need to justify yourself beyond that.

THE *SOFT* WAY FORWARD

Once you begin practicing the art of setting boundaries, you'll uncover something surprisingly beautiful: the joy of saying no. Not the guilt-ridden, second-guessing kind of no, but the confident, self-honoring kind. Every time you say no with compassion, you're actually saying yes to something else: your peace of mind, your family, your health, your purpose.

Saying no is a declaration of clarity. It creates space—space to breathe, to be present, to invest in what truly matters. It reminds you that your time and energy are precious resources, and that you get to choose where they go. It shifts your life from reaction to intention.

In *SOFT*, we understand that boundaries aren't barriers; they are bridges to wholeness. They're how we stay connected to ourselves while still loving and supporting others. They're how we protect our happiness, prevent burnout, and show up fully in the places that need us most.

So, the next time someone asks for your time, your energy, or your presence, pause. Ask yourself: Does this align with what matters most to me? If not, say no with grace, with love, and without apology. Celebrate the freedom that comes from honoring your boundaries. And trust that in doing so, you are living in alignment with your true self—strong, optimistic, and triumphantly *SOFT*.

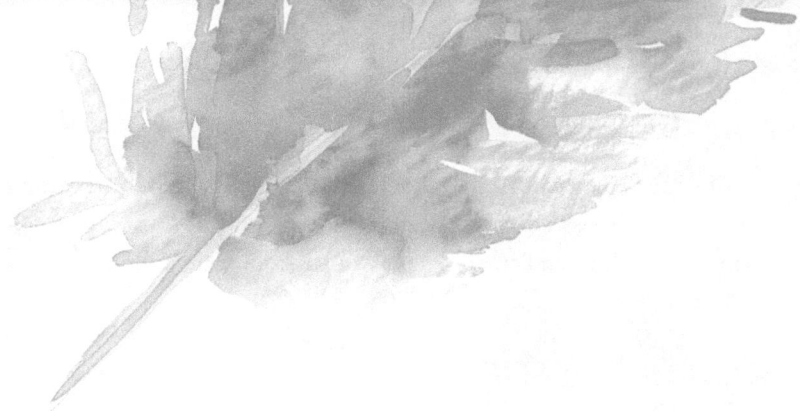

CHAPTER EIGHT

Navigating Relationships—*SOFT*ness as Strength in Love and Friendship

B ECAUSE STRENGTH IS often equated with being tough, distant, or unbreakable, it can feel counterintuitive to approach our most intimate relationships—whether romantic, familial, or platonic—with *SOFT*ness. In *SOFT: Stoically Optimistic Females Triumph*, *SOFT*ness is not only a strength, but also the very foundation of genuine, lasting connection. When it comes to love and friendship, *SOFT*ness allows us to show up authentically, build trust, and foster deeper connections. It is in our vulnerability, empathy, and gentleness that true strength resides.

So, how do we navigate our personal relationships using the principles of *SOFT*? Whether you're building a romantic partnership, a family dynamic, or a friendship, bringing *SOFT*ness into these connections doesn't mean sacrificing your boundaries or power. Instead, it means showing up fully as yourself: open-hearted, compassionate, and strong in your willingness to be real. Let's explore how *SOFTness* can transform relationships and create spaces of deeper love and mutual respect.

REDEFINING *SOFTNESS* IN RELATIONSHIPS

SOFTness is often mistaken for passivity or weakness, especially in relationships where we might fear being hurt or taken advantage of. When in reality, *SOFTness* is about vulnerability, which requires immense courage. It requires allowing yourself to be seen, to express your emotions, and to nurture meaningful connections without wearing the armor of invulnerability. *SOFTness* in relationships means showing up wholeheartedly and with sincerity—offering your care and presence while still honoring your boundaries and staying true to who you are.

In love and friendship, *SOFTness* allows us to create safe spaces for others to be themselves. It invites emotional intimacy, openness, and the kind of trust that makes relationships thrive. By tapping into *SOFTness* we can have honest conversations, work through conflict, and show compassion, not just for others but also for ourselves.

SOFTness doesn't mean avoiding difficult conversations or always being agreeable. It means demonstrating empathy, listening deeply, and communicating your needs with kindness. It means standing strong in your boundaries, while also being open to the needs and emotions of others. It's the balance of being both gentle and assertive, nurturing and firm, vulnerable and confident.

SOFTNESS IN ROMANCE

Romantic relationships are often seen as the ultimate test of vulnerability. When we fall in love, we expose parts of ourselves that we might otherwise keep hidden—our fears, our hopes, our insecurities. This level of vulnerability can be terrifying, but it's also what makes love so powerful.

In a society that sometimes encourages us to play games or keep our guard up, being *SOFT* in a romantic relationship can feel risky. But when we approach love with *SOFTness*, we create the space for true intimacy to grow. *SOFTness* in love means being willing to express how you feel, even when it's uncomfortable. It means allowing yourself to lean into trust, even when past experiences may have made you cautious. It requires nurturing the relationship with patience, communication, and compassion, even in difficult times.

It's also important to recognize that strength in a relationship isn't about controlling or dominating the other person. In a partnership, both people should feel safe enough to be vulnerable, to share their struggles, and to lean on each other. When both partners embrace *SOFTness*, the relationship becomes a place of mutual growth and support, rather than a battleground for control or ego.

For example, imagine a moment of conflict in a relationship—a misunderstanding or disagreement that could easily escalate into anger or defensiveness. *SOFTness* in this instance looks like pausing, taking a breath, and choosing to listen rather than react. Instead of speaking with defensiveness, try saying, "I hear you, and I want to understand where you're coming from." This doesn't mean ignoring your own feelings or avoiding the issue. It means approaching the conversation with empathy and a desire to resolve the conflict together.

*SOFT*ness in Friendship

Friendship, like any other relationship, requires effort, understanding, and patience. As we move through different stages of life, our friendships evolve. Some friendships deepen, while others may fade or shift. Navigating these changes with *SOFTness* helps us honor the relationships that truly matter while allowing space for growth and change.

SOFTness in friendship means being present for the people who matter to you, offering support without judgment, and giving them the freedom to be their authentic selves. It may include celebrating each other's successes, offering a listening ear during tough times, and knowing when to step back to give space when needed.

One of the most beautiful aspects of *SOFTness* in friendship is the ability to be vulnerable with each other. In an environment that often celebrates independence and self-reliance, friendships are the spaces where we can let our guard down, ask for help, and share our struggles. *SOFTness* in friendship creates a foundation of trust that allows for honest conversations about the hard stuff, whether it's navigating personal challenges, relationship difficulties, or simply feeling overwhelmed.

At the same time, *SOFTness* doesn't mean being a people-pleaser or saying yes to everything. Just as in romantic relationships, *SOFTness* in friendship requires boundaries. It includes understanding when to say no, when to take time for yourself, and when to communicate your own needs. A truly strong friendship is one where both people feel comfortable expressing themselves and setting healthy limits without fear of losing the connection.

SOFTNESS IN FAMILY RELATIONSHIPS

Family can be our greatest source of love and, sometimes, our deepest source of internal tension. In these relationships, where history runs deep and expectations often go unspoken, showing up with *SOFTness* takes courage. It's easy to compare, to feel like you're falling short, or to retreat when emotions get heavy. But in these tender spaces, *SOFTness* becomes a quiet strength—one that allows us to hold compassion for both ourselves and others, even when our stories look different.

As a single mother of two, navigating family relationships can some-times feel like walking a tightrope. I love my family dearly, but there are times when my heart tugs with an ache I can't ignore, especially when I'm around relatives who look like they have it all. The ones with the picture-perfect marriages, the kids who appear effortlessly well-behaved, and the seemingly unshakable lives. I don't begrudge them their happiness, but as someone who once dreamed of having a traditional family unit, their reality can sometimes cast a shadow on my own.

I brought my children to a large family reunion, determined to make it a fun day for all of us. As I sat at a table with family members, watching spouses exchange loving glances while their children played together without a care, I felt an unexpected wave of bitterness rise within me. *Why couldn't I have that? Why does it seem so easy for them?*

But then, I caught myself. I realized that letting these feelings fester would do nothing but pull me away from the joy of the day and the deeper connections I wanted to nurture. I took a deep breath and chose a different path: *SOFTness.*

Instead of letting my emotions isolate me, I leaned into empathy. I reminded myself that while their lives seemed perfect on the surface, I didn't know the full story. I thought about how much I valued the bond I shared with my family and how their happiness didn't diminish my own worth or my children's.

I struck up a conversation, asking them about the joys and chal-lenges of parenting and sharing some of my own stories. We laughed, swapped tips, and bonded in a way we hadn't in years. By choosing to approach them with openness and vulnerability, I was able to move past the comparisons and into a space of connection.

Later, as the kids played, a family member turned to me and said, "You're so strong. I don't know how you do it all as a single mom, but your kids are lucky to have you." Their words caught me off guard but also reminded me of something important: The strength I bring to my family is unique and valuable, even if it looks different from everyone else's contributions.

This experience taught me that *SOFTness* in relationships starts with compassion for ourselves and for others. It would have been easy to harden my heart, to retreat into resentment or envy, but instead, I chose vulnerability. By acknowledging my feelings without letting them define the interaction, I was able to reconnect with my family and strengthen our relationship.

Navigating family dynamics can be challenging, especially when surrounded by what feels like an unattainable ideal. But choosing *SOFTness*—openness, empathy, and a willingness to connect—can transform those moments of tension into opportunities for deeper understanding and growth.

SOFTness doesn't mean ignoring your emotions or pretending everything is fine. It means approaching relationships with a willingness to see beyond appearances and to value connection over comparison. It recognizes that every family has its own struggles, joys, and unique dynamics, and that your journey, no matter how different, is just as valid and meaningful.

The next time you find yourself feeling isolated or comparing your life to other people's, pause. Take a deep breath, lean into your *SOFTness*, and remind yourself that relationships are about connection, not competition. By choosing empathy and vulnerability, you create space for authentic bonds to grow, enriching your life and the lives of those around you, despite the obstacles.

Navigating Challenges with *SOFTness*

Every relationship—whether romantic or platonic—will face issues that are difficult to resolve. Whether it's a disagreement, a period of distance, or a significant life change, these moments can test the strength of your connection. *SOFTness*, however, is what allows you to navigate these challenges with grace.

When conflict arises, approaching it with *SOFTness* means being willing to listen, to understand, and to find a resolution that honors both your needs and the needs of the other person. Stay open to the possibility of growth, even when the situation feels difficult or uncomfortable. *SOFTness* allows you to move through challenges without hardening your heart or shutting down emotionally.

It's important to remember that *SOFTness* is not synonymous with weakness. In fact, it's often the *SOFTer*, more vulnerable approach that requires the most strength. It takes courage to say, "I don't have all the answers," or "I'm feeling hurt, but I want to work through this together." This kind of vulnerability invites connection and fosters trust, even in the midst of conflict.

Putting *SOFTness* into Practice in Relationships

How can you begin to bring more *SOFTness* into your closest relationships? Whether you're navigating love, friendship, or family, here are a few action points to help you embody the *SOFT* way in your personal connections:

1. *Lead with Curiosity, Not Judgment:* When tension arises or someone's behavior confuses you, pause and ask yourself what they might be going through. *SOFTness* starts with curiosity—offering the benefit of the doubt and creating room for understanding.

2. *Say What You Feel, Not Just What Sounds Good:* Vulnerability builds connection. Instead of masking your true emotions to keep

the peace, share how you really feel with kindness and clarity. Let others see the real you.

3. *Celebrate Differences:* In any relationship, differences in communication style, love language, or life choices are inevitable. *SOFTness* means appreciating those differences rather than resisting them.

4. *Respond Instead of React:* When a moment of conflict arises, take a breath before responding. A thoughtful pause can de-escalate tension and open the door to more productive, empathetic dialogue.

5. *Give Grace to Others and to Yourself:* Relationships aren't perfect, and neither are people. Offer forgiveness, patience, and understanding not only to those you care about, but also to yourself as you navigate life's complexities. *SOFTness* isn't just something we offer others. It's something we practice for ourselves, especially in those moments when comparison and self-judgment start to take hold.

THE *SOFT* WAY FORWARD

Living the *SOFT* way means embracing *SOFTness* not just in your personal life, but in all your relationships. Show up with empathy, openness, and vulnerability, while also maintaining the strength of your boundaries and self-respect. *SOFTness* allows you to build relationships that are based on mutual trust, love, and respect, rather than power dynamics or control.

Whether in love or friendship, *SOFTness* invites us to be fully present, to communicate with kindness, and to create spaces where both we and the people we care about can grow. It's the strength to be real, to show up as we are, and to allow others to do the same.

As you navigate your relationships, remember that *SOFTness* is not a weakness, it's a source of incredible strength. It's what allows you to love fully, to support deeply, and to build connections that last. So, embrace the *SOFTness* within you, and let it guide you toward relationships that uplift, nurture, and empower you and the people you care about.

In love and in friendship, *SOFTness* is not the absence of strength, it's the quiet, steady force that makes relationships thrive.

CHAPTER NINE

SOFT Self-Care— Recharging Without Guilt

S ELF-CARE. IT'S A term we hear often, yet many women still carry a quiet discomfort when it comes up. We're praised for sacrifice and selflessness, but rarely for slowing down. In a world that celebrates hustle, overextension, and being "always on," taking a moment for yourself can feel indulgent or even irresponsible. But here's the truth that we live by in *SOFT: Stoically Optimistic Females Triumph*: Self-care isn't selfish. It's survival. And even more important than that—it's strategy.

Living the *SOFT* way means recognizing that our well-being isn't a side project. It's the foundation of everything else. When we care for ourselves, we amplify our ability to care for others, to lead with presence, and to walk through life with clarity and strength.

REFRAMING THE ROLE OF SELF-CARE

Self-care isn't always grand. It's not reserved for spa days or weekend retreats (though those are lovely). Sometimes, it's as simple—and powerful—as saying no to another obligation, taking a walk in the fresh air, or pausing to breathe when your calendar feels like it's closing in on you. It's about returning to yourself, consistently and compassionately.

For years, I balanced the beautiful chaos of career, parenting, community leadership, and volunteer work. I thrived in the fullness of it, but the pace came at a cost. I was tired physically, emotionally, and spiritually. My calendar was full, but my cup was empty.

And yet, whenever I tried to carve out time for myself, guilt would creep in. A hot yoga class, a solo run, or even a few quiet minutes with a book felt like time stolen from someone else—my kids, my parents, my purpose. I worried that stepping away to care for myself might look self-indulgent.

But then came the crash. My body made the decision for me, and I was overcome by fatigue, irritability, and disconnection. I wasn't showing up the way I wanted to in my life, because I was showing up last for myself.

That realization was the turning point.

One morning, after a string of sleepless nights and a calendar packed tighter than my lungs in a yoga twist, I stood in my kitchen watching my kids laugh at breakfast, and I felt—nothing. Not joy. Not presence. Just a blank space. That scared me.

Later that day, my dad—gentle, observant—asked, "When's the last time you went to hot yoga?"

His words weren't an accusation. They were a reminder. He knew I'm my most grounded, loving self when I'm caring for myself first. That evening, I booked the class. I showed up on the mat. And by the time I walked through the door afterward, my kids noticed immediately: "You seem happy, Mom." And I was.

Understanding the Cultural Roots of Guilt

Before we can let go of guilt, we must name where it comes from. Many of us were raised in cultures—including family, military, or faith traditions—that taught us to give without stopping. To be good meant to be available. To be strong meant to keep pushing. And to pause? That felt like failure.

We learned to prioritize everyone else's needs while quietly silencing our own. Whether through military conditioning, spiritual teachings, or generational modeling, we internalized the idea that our worth was tied to output. That exhaustion equaled devotion.

These messages weren't born from malice; they were born from survival. From generations of women who held families, communities, and missions together through sheer will. But what served them in one season may not serve us in this one.

It's time to rewrite the narrative.

True endurance isn't found in the hustle—it's built in the pause. And no, that doesn't mean a luxurious retreat or expensive self-care routines. It means showing up consistently for yourself. It means carving out space to breathe, reflect, and reset, because when you are grounded, you are powerful.

Guilt may be the ghost of old expectations, but grace is the gift we give ourselves when we choose presence over performance. When we stop measuring our worth by how much we've done and start honoring who we are while doing it.

So how do we begin to release guilt's grip?

Letting Go of the Guilt

Guilt is one of the most persistent barriers to self-care. It whispers that you're being selfish. That others need you more. That your worth is measured by your output.

But here's what I've learned: Guilt is not your guide. It's a signal to pause and check in.

Instead of asking, "Am I doing enough?" ask, "Am I caring for myself as well as I care for others?"

That question will quiet the noise and bring you back to your truth.

I remember a Saturday morning when I left the dishes in the sink and went for a thirty-minute run. I felt the tug of responsibility pulling me back, but I kept going. When I returned, nothing had fallen apart. But everything inside me had realigned. I was grounded, clear, and fully available to the people I love.

That's what self-care really is: not escape, but restoration.

Embracing Self-Care as Essential

Recharging without guilt means seeing self-care not as an afterthought but as a core part of your life. It means recognizing that your well-being matters, and that taking care of yourself is not a selfish act—it's a gift to yourself and to those around you.

Here are a few techniques to help you practice self-care the *SOFT* way:

1. *Shift Your Mindset:* The first step in recharging without guilt is changing the way you think about self-care. Instead of viewing it as something extra or indulgent, start seeing self-care as a necessity. Remind yourself that you deserve care just as much as anyone else. This isn't about "earning" time for yourself; it's about honoring your inherent worth and the importance of your well-being.

2. *Create a Self-Care Routine:* Self-care is most effective when it's consistent. Rather than waiting until you're overwhelmed to take a break, make self-care a regular part of your routine. This could be as simple as setting aside a few minutes each day for quiet reflection, stretching, journaling, or reading. The key is to find activities that genuinely replenish you and to regularly incorporate them into your life.

3. *Prioritize Rest:* Rest is one of the most underrated forms of self-care, yet it's also one of the most essential. In a world that glorifies busyness, rest can feel like a radical act of self-respect. Give yourself permission to rest without guilt, whether that means taking a nap, sleeping in, or simply enjoying a moment of stillness. Remember, rest is not a reward. It's a requirement for a healthy, balanced life.

4. *Set Boundaries to Protect Your Time:* In addition to the activities you do for yourself, self-care includes the boundaries you set to protect your time and energy. This might mean saying no to extra commitments, carving out time for solitude, or limiting social engagements when you need time to recharge. Boundaries allow you to protect your well-being and ensure that you have the energy to show up fully in the areas that matter most.

5. *Listen to Your Body and Mind:* One of the most powerful ways to practice self-care is to tune in to your own needs. Our bodies and minds are constantly giving us signals about what they need, whether it's rest, movement, connection, or solitude. The more you practice listening to yourself, the easier it becomes to respond with compassion and care. Trust your instincts, and honor what your body and mind are telling you.

The *SOFT* Way Forward

In *SOFT,* we believe that self-care is not just about surviving, it's about thriving. When you prioritize your own well-being, you create a strong foundation from which every other aspect of your life can flourish. Self-care allows you to be present, engaged, and thankful in all that you do. It gives you the resilience to face challenges, the clarity to make decisions, and the strength to pursue your dreams.

Remember, self-care is not a privilege reserved for certain moments; it's an essential part of a balanced, fulfilling life. When you give yourself permission to recharge without guilt, you embrace a life that honors your needs and respects your boundaries. You show yourself, and the world, that you are worthy of care, rest, and joy.

So let go of the guilt. Embrace self-care as an act of self-love, self-respect, and self-preservation. Prioritize your well-being without apology, knowing that when you care for yourself, you're able to live the *SOFT* way—fully, authentically, and powerfully.

CHAPTER TEN

UNAPOLOGETICALLY *SOFT*— OWN YOUR STORY

WE'VE REACHED A powerful part of our journey together. This is the point where you stand in the fullness of who you are, without apology, without shrinking, and without hesitation. Be unapologetically *SOFT* and embrace your authentic self with pride. Own your story—all of it: the triumphs, the setbacks, the awkwardness, the vulnerability, the strength. *SOFT* is a commitment to living your truth with courage, compassion, and a steadfast belief that you are enough just as you are.

In a society that often asks you to mold yourself to fit specific expectations, standing confidently in your own story is a radical act. Owning who you are—your experiences, your values, and your unique perspective—means freeing yourself from the need to conform to someone else's definition of success or strength. Live authentically, make decisions that honor your values, and embrace your journey with pride.

Celebrating your story and embodying the *SOFT* philosophy as a way of life is showing up in the world as your true self, empowered by your experiences and grounded in your unique blend of optimism, resilience, and compassion.

Embrace Your Authenticity

Authenticity is often celebrated but not always understood. Being authentic doesn't mean revealing every aspect of yourself to everyone or sharing your struggles with the world. Rather, it is knowing who you are and having the courage to live in alignment with that truth. Authenticity means letting go of the need for approval and giving yourself permission to be exactly who you are.

Owning your story means embracing your complexity, contradictions, and evolution. You don't have to fit into one mold, one identity, or one narrative. You can be a leader and a nurturer, strong and vulnerable, *SOFT* and assertive. You are allowed to grow, to change, and to embody all parts of yourself. Authenticity is fluid, and it's yours to define.

Living authentically also means that you don't have to explain or justify yourself to others. When you own your story, you free yourself from the need to gain external validation. Your worth isn't determined by other people's opinions or expectations, it's defined by your inner sense of self. This is what it means to be unapologetically *SOFT*: You show up as you are, without apology, knowing that your authenticity is your strength.

For example, a comment I often hear is, "You're always so busy!" Sometimes it's said with admiration, sometimes with concern, and occasionally with a hint of disdain. "Do you ever slow down?" "Do you make time for yourself?" "When's the last time you took a real vacation?" The questions are usually well-meaning, but they often come with an undertone that suggests I might be doing too much, or that I'm somehow neglecting myself or others in the process.

I used to let those questions get to me. I'd wonder, *Am I doing too much? Should I be scaling back? Am I missing out on the chance to rest or take a step back from it all?* Then I reflect on how I actually feel about my life. The truth is, I don't feel overwhelmed or regretful about the way I choose to live—I feel alive.

Yes, I juggle a lot. Between my career, volunteer work, community engagements, raising two children as a single mom, and carving out time for myself, my days are full. But they're also *mine*. Every piece of my life is something I've chosen because it aligns with who I am and what I value. I've learned to navigate my commitments with intention, and I've found a rhythm that works for me.

I love waking up early for a morning run, even when it means sacrificing a little extra sleep. That time outdoors, moving my body and clearing my mind, feels like a gift to myself. I treasure my moments in hot yoga, where the heat and the flow of the practice remind me to breathe deeply and reconnect with my body. These activities might look like "too much" to others, but for me, they're essential. They're what allow me to live fully in every other area of my life.

And then there's the joy I find in everything else. Speaking at community events, mentoring others, showing up for my kids' activities, and giving back to causes I care about all fuel me. To outsiders, it might seem like I'm constantly "on," but to me, it feels like living my truth. I love my life, and I love how full it is.

The key to being unapologetically *SOFT* is knowing what matters most to you and owning it without hesitation. For me, that means recognizing that my full schedule isn't a burden, it's a reflection of the life I've chosen to build. When people question whether I make time for myself, I smile because I know I do. Running, yoga, reading, spending time with my children are all parts of my self-care, woven into the fabric of my life. I don't have to justify it, explain it, or seek validation for how I choose to spend my time.

Living unapologetically also means letting go of the pressure to meet everyone's expectations. I don't need to scale back or live smaller just because others think I should. My life is a balance of commitments, passions, and care for myself and my family. It's a balance that works for me, and that's all that matters.

The next time someone says to you, "You're always so busy," or "You do too much," pause and ask yourself: Do I love the life I'm living? Does it reflect my values and priorities? Am I making time for what matters most to me? If the answers are yes, then own it. Smile and say, "I love my life, and I'm living it to the fullest."

The Power of Owning Your Story

Owning your story isn't only empowering for you, it's also a gift to others. When you stand in your truth, you give those around you permission to do the same. By embracing your experiences, values, and unique journey, you become an example of what it means to live authentically. You show others that they, too, can be fully themselves without shame or fear of judgment.

Your story holds immense power. It's a testament to the strength, resilience, and wisdom you've cultivated along the way. Every experience—every triumph, every challenge—has shaped who you are. Owning your story means honoring those experiences and acknowledging the growth they've brought into your life. It means recognizing that you are whole and complete, not in spite of your journey but because of it.

Owning your story also frees you from the weight of comparison. When you are grounded in your truth, you no longer feel the need to measure yourself against others. You understand that your journey is uniquely yours and that there is no "right" way to live, succeed, or thrive. You are exactly where you're meant to be, and that is enough.

Let Go of the Need for Approval

One of the greatest barriers to living unapologetically is the need for approval. We often feel pressure to meet others' expectations, to be "likable," or to gain validation from outside sources. But seeking approval keeps us from living authentically and from making choices that honor who we truly are. The need for approval can lead us to silence our voice, compromise our values, and suppress our desires.

To be unapologetically *SOFT* is to release the need for approval. It's about trusting that you are enough as you are, without external validation. Letting go of this need does not dismiss others' opinions entirely, but it gives you the power to choose whose voices you listen to. It's about knowing that your self-worth isn't dependent on others' acceptance.

When you let go of the need for approval, you create space to live fully in your truth. You become free to pursue what makes you happy, to speak your mind, and to follow your own path. You are no longer bound by others' expectations; instead, you are guided by your own values, desires, and dreams.

Practicing Self-Compassion

Owning your story also means practicing self-compassion. Along the way, you may face doubts, insecurities, or moments of self-criticism. You may be tempted to dwell on past mistakes or feel ashamed of certain parts of your journey. But self-compassion is essential to living unapologetically. It's about treating yourself with the same kindness, understanding, and forgiveness that you would offer to a friend.

Self-compassion allows you to accept your imperfections without judgment. It's the understanding that you are human, that you will make mistakes, and that those mistakes do not define you. When you embrace self-compassion, you create a foundation of inner support that allows you to stand tall in your truth, even on difficult days.

To practice self-compassion, start by being gentle with yourself. Acknowledge your efforts, celebrate your progress, and forgive yourself for any perceived shortcomings. Remember that you are constantly growing, and that every step—no matter how small—is a testament to your resilience and strength.

Live the *SOFT* Way: Be Unapologetically You

Remember that being unapologetically *SOFT* is about embracing the journey of becoming your truest self. Understand that *SOFTness*, optimism, resilience, and compassion are not traits you have to defend or justify. They are your power, your essence, and the foundation of a fulfilling, authentic life.

To live unapologetically is to commit to your own happiness, to honor your needs, and to pursue your passions without waiting for permission from others. Celebrate who you are, embrace your individuality, and trust that you are worthy of a life that reflects your values and desires.

As you move forward, carry this commitment with you:

1. *Embrace Your Fullness:* You don't have to squeeze into a single role, label, or identity. You are multi-faceted, complex, and whole. Embrace every part of yourself—your strengths, your *SOFTness*, your triumphs, and your challenges. These are what make you uniquely you.

2. *Speak Your Truth:* Living unapologetically means standing in your truth, even when it feels vulnerable. Speak up for what you believe

in, express your needs, and share your story. Your voice is powerful, and it deserves to be heard.

3. *Follow Your Path*: Trust your intuition, follow your passions, and pursue the life that resonates with you. You don't have to conform to others' expectations or follow a path that doesn't align with your heart. Your journey is yours to define.

4. *Celebrate Your Journey*: Own your story with pride, knowing that every step, every lesson, and every experience has shaped who you are. Celebrate your growth, honor your resilience, and remember that you are exactly where you need to be.

THE *SOFT* WAY FORWARD

To live as an unapologetically *SOFT* woman is to embody strength in a way that honors your authentic self. It's about being resilient without hardening, compassionate without losing yourself, and confident without needing validation. Living the *SOFT* way acknowledges that you are worthy, your journey is valuable, and you are enough, just as you are.

So, here's to owning your story. Here's to living with courage, kindness, and unwavering self-respect. Here's to being unapologetically *you*, and to creating a life that reflects the fullness of your heart and soul.

Because here's the truth: The *SOFT* movement isn't just about you or me—it's about all of us. It's about creating a culture where authenticity is admired, vulnerability is respected, and compassion is recognized as power. As you leave these pages, I hope you see yourself not just as a reader of this book, but as a voice in this movement. The world doesn't need more perfection—it needs more presence. It needs you to show up fully and freely.

And so, I leave you with this: Don't just *read SOFT*. *Live* it. Carry it into your relationships, your workplace, your community. Let it manifest itself in your decisions, in your boundaries, and in the way you speak to yourself when no one else is listening. Let your *SOFTness* be your revolution—and your legacy.

In every moment, remember: You are *SOFT*, and that is your strength.

CHAPTER ELEVEN

The *SOFT* Legacy

A S WE REACH the end of this journey together, take a moment to reflect on what it means to live as a *SOFT* woman. *Stoically Optimistic Females Triumph* is more than a philosophy—it's a movement of strength, compassion, and authenticity that you carry forward with every choice, every relationship, and every moment of courage. Embracing the *SOFT* way of life is a commitment to showing up fully as you are, grounded in self-respect and a deep sense of purpose.

Living the *SOFT* way means finding strength in places where it's often overlooked. Recognize the power of your vulnerability, the wisdom in your optimism, and the quiet strength in your empathy and grace. We are often pushed to be harder, tougher, or more cynical, so choosing *SOFTness* is a courageous act of defiance. It's a statement that you can be resilient without becoming hardened, optimistic without becoming naive, and powerful without sacrificing your gentleness.

The legacy of *SOFT* is a life lived on your terms. It includes being fully engaged with your own story, embracing all the beautiful, messy, and complex parts of who you are. It's about giving yourself permission to grow, to evolve, and to show up authentically in every aspect of your life. When you live the *SOFT* way, you honor your self-care, set compassionate boundaries, and cultivate relationships that uplift and nourish yourself and others. You lead with empathy, recharge without guilt, and own your story unapologetically.

A World Transformed by *SOFT*ness

Imagine a world where more people lived the *SOFT* way—a world where strength is redefined to include compassion, optimism is seen as resilience, and empathy guides our interactions. This is the legacy you contribute to by embracing the *SOFT* philosophy. Each act of vulnerability, each moment of self-care, and each empathetic connection leaves a ripple effect, inspiring others to live more authentically and compassionately.

The *SOFT* legacy is one of courage, integrity, and heart. It's a life lived boldly, not because you have all the answers, but because you are willing to keep learning, growing, and showing up as your true self. The legacy of *SOFT* is yours to shape and carry forward, and it's one that will continue to evolve as you do.

Carrying the *SOFT* Legacy Forward

Remember that the goal of living the *SOFT* way isn't to achieve perfection. The goal is to embrace who you are by honoring your journey. There will be times when you feel the pressure to conform or moments when self-doubt creeps in. But the *SOFT* philosophy is a reminder that you have everything you need within you to navigate life with grace, resilience, and purpose. Here are a few principles to carry with you as you continue living the *SOFT* way:

1. *Choose Vulnerability as Strength:* Embrace vulnerability as a source of connection and courage. Show up with your whole self, knowing that authenticity builds the deepest relationships and the truest legacy. Your willingness to be seen and to share your story will inspire others to do the same.

2. *Stay Optimistic Amid Challenges:* Hold on to hope, even in the face of uncertainty. Optimism does not mean ignoring difficulties; it means believing in your capacity to grow through them. Your optimism will light the way not only for yourself but also for those around you.

3. *Lead with Empathy:* Approach others with compassion, understanding, and respect. Empathy is the quiet power that creates lasting impact. By leading with empathy, you foster trust, build stronger connections, and create an environment where people feel valued.

4. *Set Boundaries with Compassion:* Remember that boundaries are essential to self-care and sustainable relationships. Protecting your time, energy, and well-being allows you to be fully present and engaged in the moments that matter most. Saying no when you need to is an act of self-respect and kindness.

5. *Own Your Story with Pride:* Your journey, with all its triumphs and setbacks, is uniquely yours. Celebrate your experiences, your growth, and the person you've become. Living unapologetically *SOFT* means standing in your truth, without shrinking, and knowing that your story is a legacy worth honoring.

LIVING THE LEGACY OUT LOUD

I didn't know how far the *SOFT* movement would ripple, until one day, I got a message from a young woman I mentored years ago during her military transition. She shared that reading the early drafts of *SOFT* gave her permission to finally embrace the parts of herself she once tried to mute—her compassion, her tears, her hopefulness. "I always thought I had to lead like everyone else—tough and guarded," she wrote. "Now, I realize I can lead like me. That's what you showed me. That's what *SOFT* gave me permission to do."

In that moment, I realized this isn't just a movement—it's a mirror we hold up to each other to remind us we are seen, we are powerful, and we are not alone. That's the legacy. It's not perfection; it's presence. What we leave behind doesn't need to shout about us because we already have a deep understanding of our worth.

But perhaps the most sacred space where the *SOFT* legacy has taken root is within my own home. Throughout the past year of writing this manuscript—now a book—my parents and children became part of the process. We'd gather in the living room, reading drafts aloud, pausing to reflect, cry, and laugh through shared memories. We shared unspoken moments about military deployments, the silence and distance that came with them. We talked about divorce, about the emotional weight of single parenting, about the ambition that pulled me forward and the guilt that sometimes held me back.

In those vulnerable moments, something powerful happened: We grew closer. We gave each other grace. My children began to understand not just what I do, but why I do it. My parents offered insight into their own sacrifices and regrets, and together we healed parts of our story that had long gone unspoken. Writing this book has not only changed me—it's transformed my family. It reminded all of us that strength isn't found in silence; it's found in the willingness to speak the truth, together.

THE *SOFT* WAY FORWARD

As you finish this book, I hope you realize that *SOFT* is not a destination—it's a movement. It's a way of living, loving, and leading with authenticity and strength. The principles of *SOFT* are yours to carry forward, to adapt, and to share with others who may need a reminder that their *SOFTness* is a source of power.

This movement doesn't end with these pages; it begins here. Every time you own your story, every time you choose empathy, every time you balance vulnerability with confidence, you are part of the *SOFT* way forward. You are proving that there is a different way to thrive: a way that doesn't demand we sacrifice our *SOFTness* in order to succeed.

Together, we are creating a world where being *SOFT* is celebrated, not questioned. A world where strength is redefined, relationships are built on authenticity, and self-care is seen as a non-negotiable act of love. This is the *SOFT* legacy, and it is one we are writing together.

So, as you step into the world unapologetically *SOFT*, know that you are not alone. You are part of a growing community of women that is changing the narrative one moment of courage, compassion, and connection at a time. Together, we will be the legacy of the *SOFT: Stoically Optimistic Females Triumph* movement as we individually own our unique journeys, trust in our strength, and let our *SOFTness* be the force that transforms the world around us, while sharing with our sisters along the way.

Take a moment now to honor yourself. You've committed to a journey, to a movement of living with authenticity, strength, and compassion. This pledge to being unapologetically *SOFT* is a triumph in itself. It's a testament to your resilience, courage, and willingness to embrace life fully, without apology, and without compromise.

Acknowledgments

Writing this book has been one of the most vulnerable, liberating, and deeply personal journeys of my life, and it would not have been possible without the love, support, and encouragement of so many remarkable people.

To my family, who have been my foundation—thank you for instilling in me the values of service, resilience, and faith. You reminded me daily that SOFTness is not a weakness but a powerful reflection of who we are and where we come from.

To the women whose stories, strength, and SOFTness have inspired every word on these pages—thank you for showing up authentically and reminding me that we are never alone in our struggles or triumphs.

To the mentors, friends, and colleagues who encouraged me to write this book, who listened when I needed to talk, and who reminded me of my "why" when the writing became difficult—your belief in me means more than you'll ever know.

To the editors, designers, and publishing team who helped bring SOFT to life—thank you for treating this book with the care, clarity, and purpose it deserves.

And finally, to every reader holding this book in your hands—thank you for saying yes to the SOFT movement. May you feel seen, heard, and empowered to lead and live with unapologetic strength and grace.

About the Author

Dr. Chaunté Hall is a U.S. Air Force OIF/OEF veteran and a life-long advocate for the military and the greater San Antonio community. Raised in a family rooted in military service, she grew up surrounded by discipline, resilience, and faith. Her parents—both Air Force veterans—instilled in her the values of humility, service, and the quiet strength that would eventually shape the SOFT movement.

Having served honorably in both active duty and reserve capacities, Dr. Hall brings firsthand understanding of the complexities of military life, including deployments, reintegration, and identity shifts. These experiences fueled her passion to co-found and serve as CEO of Centurion Military Alliance (CMA), a nonprofit dedicated to equipping transitioning military families through education, vocational readiness, and holistic support.

Dr. Hall currently serves as an executive in the City of San Antonio and as an adjunct professor, where she helps bridge the gap between military, education, and industry. She is also the visionary behind *SOFT: Stoically Optimistic Females Triumph*, a movement and book empowering women to lead with authenticity, vulnerability, and strength.

In addition to her executive leadership roles, Dr. Hall is a committed board member across several nonprofit organizations, advocating for youth development, military support, and education access.

Above all, her greatest and most cherished title is mother to her beloved son and daughter who continue to inspire her to live with purpose and lead with heart.